# *All letters, Applications, Business Letters and Business Email*

## *Book Six*

### *By*

## *Professor Rama Shankar Shukla*

*Dedicated*

*To*

*My Parents*

*Whose Blessings*

*I*

*Always*

*Seek!*

# How to use this book?

*This book contains letters and application mostly in complete block format, However, some letters have been repeated in image format so that you are able to see their correct format.*

# Disclaimer

# Part 1
## *Introduction to Letter Writing*

*This*

*Part*

*Contains*

*Classification*

*Of*

*Letters*

# Letter Writing

Of all the forms of written communication, letter writing is most common and agreeable.

It is as common to all as talking on the phone or chatting with friends. Once or twice, you must have written letters to your friends or relatives.

A letter is a piece of writing on a paper addressed to a person to give some information. A letter is generally written on a piece of paper and put inside an envelope on which the name and address of the person, who has to receive the related information, is written.

A postal stamp is affixed on the envelope and then it is dropped in the letter box from where it is collected by the employees from the post office. The envelope is then sent to the address written on it by the postal department.

Some private courier companies also do this job. They take some money for this work. The government postal department takes this money in the form of a postal ticket which we affix on the envelope.

Although the frequency of letter writing has rather decreased since the advent of telephone and internet (E-mail) yet its importance as documented record/ evidence cannot be denied.

There are various types of letters that we write in our daily life. We write letters to our friends and relatives, to various government departments, to firms, dealers and so on.

The types are many.

However, we can categorize the letters broadly into two categories.

1. Formal Letters
2. Informal Letters

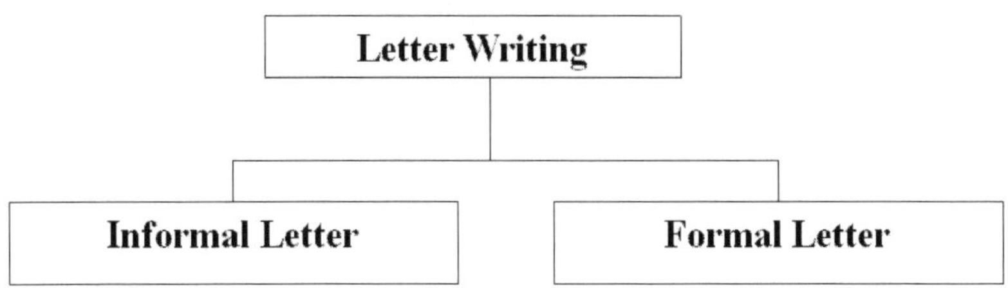


# Informal Letter

All the letters that we write to the people with whom we have an informal relationship e.g. our friends and relatives (father, mother, uncle, aunt, sister, brother etc.) are called informal letters.

# Formal Letter

All the letters that we write to the people with whom we have a formal relationship e.g. the head of an institution/ a government organization/business organization etc. come under the category of formal letters.

These are the letters that we address to the Principal of a school, the head of a government office, or the head of an office belonging to a business organization or an office bearer. All the business letters are formal letters.

# Part 2

# *Informal Letters*

*This part
Contains
The letters
That we write
To
Our family members,
Relatives
Or
Our friends*

# The Lay Out of an Informal Letter (Why is Lay Out necessary?)

An informal letter is very much familiar to you. I am sure that you must have written such a letter in your life. However, not all people are able to write a letter in the correct format. When they write a letter, they don't care for format or layout of the letter. They would write a piece of information not in the right place decided for it but anywhere they like. You must know it is the lay out or the letter that distinguishes a letter from other types of documents. Lay out or format means it tells you what information is to be placed where. Remember that lay out has been decided as per most common practice. Exceptionally, it may differ if the people of a place have adopted a different practice. For your convenience, the layout of an informal letter is given on the next page. It will tell you what to write and where. You can follow the layout and write an informal letter easily.

| | **1. Return Address** |

| | **2. Date……..** |

**3. Salutation** e.g. Dear father/Dear friend etc

**4. Main body of the letter**

.......................................................................................
.......................................................................................
.......................................................................................
.......................................................................................
.......................................................................................
.......................................................................................
.......................................................................................
.......................................................................................
...........................................

**5. Complimentary Close** e.g. Yours sincerely/Yours affectionately

**6. Signature**

1. ***Return Address-***

This is the address of the letter writer (sender). See figure no 1 and write the address of your residence at place no 1. In other words, the writer of the letter (sender) writes the address of his/her residence here.

2. ***Date-***

Under the address, the date of writing the letter is written. Usually the date should be written in the following manner e.g. 14 October, 2003 or 14 Oct, 2003. You can write 14/10/2003 or 14-10-2003 also but if you spell the name of the month, it is always a safe choice because in some countries people write the name of the month first and date latter and in some countries date first and month latter; and thus, your date may be ambiguous. In other words, 4-3-2003 may be read as 4 March, 2003 and 3 April, 2003 both.

3. ***Salutation-***

Salutation is the respectful beginning of the letter. You begin writing the letter with some informal address like Dear friend or Dear father. Never write full names here but use some informal word of address by which you usually call your or relative e.g. Dear Dad, Dear Mom, Dear Monu, Dear Pinky, Dear father, Dear brother, Dear sister etc. This portion of the letter is called salutation. It is written at place no.3 (see figure no. 1)

## 4. *Main Body-*

Your message is the main body of the letter, which contains all the important information. It is the place you write about real business concerned. It is place no.4 in figure 1. People generally start the main body of the letter in the following way: - "I am quite well here and hope for the same to you." Or "I am quite fine here and hope for the same to you." or

"I am quite fine here and hope that this letter of mine finds you in the best of your health and cheerful mood" This is right. If you have any other version, that is also welcome. Or if you like you may come directly on the point here. But remember if there has been a tragic incident at your friend's home, you should not write the above-mentioned sentences. However, you should start it in the following way: - "I am very sorry to know that..." "I am awfully sorry to know that.............." or "I am extremely sorry to know that...................."

## 5. *Complimentary Close-*

We end the letter by a complimentary close. In other words, it is a respectful ending of the letter. It consists of some words of compliment e.g. "Yours sincerely", "Yours lovingly", "Yours affectionately". Write "Yours affectionately", "Your loving son/daughter" to the members of your family and "Yours sincerely" or "Your loving friend" to your friend. Remember that the first letter of the complimentary close must be capital. You can write "Yours sincerely" or "Sincerely yours". Both are correct. You can also write "Regards" or "Best regards" or "Kind regards" or "With best wishes" or "Sincerely" whichever you find suitable. There is another set of complimentary closes e.g. "Yours forever" or "Warms regards" or "With warm regards" which will depend upon your relation with the receiver of the letter. Think about your relation with the receiver of the letter then decide a suitable complimentary close for ending your letter. Complimentary close is written at place no 5. (See figure no 1)

## 6. *Signature-*

You put down your signature and name at the end of your letter under Complimentary Close at place no 6. (See figure no 1)

# *Specimen Letters*

### (Specimen no 1 - <u>A letter to father</u>)

Sardar Patel Hostel
University of Allahabad
26 February,2005

Dear Daddy,

I am quite fine here and hope that this letter of mine finds you in the best of your health and cheerful mood. I hope that Mom and Dolly too are happy and cheerful.

My examinations are going to start from 15 March 2005. I am well prepared for the examination. Besides this, I hope that I shall be able to cross the preliminary examination of IAS in my first attempt.

My teacher has suggested some more good books which are useful for some papers of final year and for IAS Examination also. Please send me Rs 500 more so that I may be able to buy these books.

Love to Mom and Dolly.

Affectionately yours,
Sudhir Agrawal

### (Specimen no 2 - <u>Letter of congratulation to friend</u>)

Rajendra Nagar Satna (MP)
26 October, 2004

Dear Ravi,

I was extremely delighted to know from the newspaper that you have topped the Pre-Medical Test 2005.

I was overwhelmed at such an amazing performance of yours. My whole family is delighted that you are first among the ten best achievers of PMT.

I congratulate you on your brilliant success. Please accept congratulations from all the members of my family.

Besides this, your arrival to our home, when you come to Satna, is most awaited.

Please do not forget it, convey my best regards to your parents.

Yours sincerely,
Vikas Gupta

(Specimen no 3-<u>A letter of condolence to your friend</u>)

Rajendra Nagar Satna(MP)<br>28 October,2005

Dear friend,

I feel extremely sorry at the sad and sudden demise of your father.

It is an infinite loss not only to you but to me as well. He has been a guide to both of us in the struggle of life. I request you not to feel alone at this hour of tragedy.

However, "Man proposes; God disposes". God's will is above all. Therefore, have faith in the Almighty. "Do thy duty; reward is not thy concern". "Whatever God does, does for good". We all are with you.

I request you to resume the charge of your duties and work with the same spirit. After all, this is all that your father really wanted from you.

We all stand by you in this hour of grief.

Yours truly,<br>Rajesh Kumar

# Style of Presentation of the Letter

You have already come to know the layout of the informal letter. However the same layout may be presented in a different pattern also. Presenting the layout of the letter in a different pattern/alignment without making changes in the order of its elements is known as the style of presentation of the letter. There are several styles of presentation. Out of them, two styles are very popular, Block Style and Complete Block Style. You can write a letter in either of the two styles. Both the styles are acceptable. In fact, the style of the letter is your personal decision in which style you would like to present your letter. In Block Style, the inside address, date, complimentary close and signature are aligned on the right side and all the other lines are aligned on the left side. In the Complete Block Style, all the lines are aligned on the left side. This style was invented after the advent of computers. This style is very easy and time saving. You will come to know about all the different styles of letters in the chapter Business Letters.

The two styles Block Style and Complete Block Style are as follows. I am presenting same letter in both the styles:

( Specimen Block Style)

**Rajendra Nagar Satna (MP)**

26 October, 2004

Dear Ravi,

I was extremely delighted to know from the newspaper that you have topped the Pre-Medical Test 2005.

I was overwhelmed at such an amazing performance of yours. My whole family is delighted that you are first among the ten best achievers of PMT.

I congratulate you on your brilliant success. Please accept congratulations from all the members of my family.

Besides this, your arrival to our home, when you come to Satna, is most awaited.

Please do not forget it, convey my best regards to your parents.

Yours sincerely,<br>Vikas Gupta

(Specimen Complete Block Style)

**Rajendra Nagar Satna (MP)**

26 October, 2004

Dear Ravi,

I was extremely delighted to know from the newspaper that you have topped the Pre-Medical Test 2005.
I was overwhelmed at such an amazing performance of yours. My whole family is delighted that you are first among the ten best achievers of PMT.
I congratulate you on your brilliant success. Please accept congratulations from all the members of my family.
Besides this, your arrival to our home, when you come to Satna, is most awaited.

Please do not forget it, convey my best regards to your parents.

Yours sincerely,
Vikas Gupta

***

# Some More Sample Informal Letters

1. Write a letter to your father asking him to send you Rs 1000 for books.
   Ans.-

   New Hostel
   Mahakaushal Convent
   Jabalpur (MP)

   22 July 2015

   Dear father,
   I am quite well here and hope for the same to you. My classes have started. Teachers are teaching us with great interest. I have bought all the books that I should.
   But my science teacher has recommended some extra books that I could not buy because I did not have enough money.
   Please send me Rs 1000 as early as possible.
   Convey my best regards to mom and love to Didi.

   Yours affectionately,
   Ravi

2. Write a letter to your father informing him about your hostel life.
   Ans.-

   New Hostel
   Mahakaushal Convent
   Jabalpur (MP)

   22 July 2015

   Dear father,

I am quite well here and hope for the same to you. My room partners are very friendly and cooperative. Our hostel warden is very kind and affectionate to us. He visits our hostel two or three times a day. He asks about our difficulties and removes them. The food of our boarding is very good. Classes have started. Our teachers are very intelligent and cooperative. You need not worry about these things.
Convey my best regards to mom and love to Didi.

Your loving son,
Deepak

3. Write a letter to your friend inviting him to your brother's marriage.
Ans.-

Bharahut Nagar
Satna (MP)

22 May 2015

Dear friend,
I am quite well here and hope for the same to you. Here is happy news for you. My elder brother is going to be married on 10 June 2015.
I invite you to the marriage ceremony of my brother. Please come with your family. I invite uncle, auntie and Didi also.
Remember your presence is most solicited. Please be here by 8 June 2015.
My best regards to your parents.

Your loving friend,

Ravi Shukla

4. Write a letter to your friend congratulating him on his success.
   Ans.-

   Rajendra Nagar
   Satna (MP)

   22 July 2015

   Dear friend,
   I was very happy to know that you stood first in the whole Satna District. I got this news through Dainik Bhaskar today. It is a beautiful reward for your hard work.
   I congratulate you on your success.
   Convey my best regards to your parents.

   Your loving friend,


   Ravi Varma

5. Write a letter to your friend inviting him to your city during summer vacation.
   Ans.-

   Bharahut Nagar
   Satna (MP)

   22 April 2015

   Dear friend,
   I am quite well here and hope for the same to you. My examinations are over. My papers have gone well. I have decided to learn spoken English and computer and during summer vacation.

I invite you to come to Satna and learn Spoken English and computer with me. Our teacher of English gives unique coaching. It is a very nice chance for us. I am sure that you will accept my offer.
Convey my best regards to your parents.

With best wishes,


Rajesh Sharma

6. Write a letter to your friend inviting him to your birthday party.
Ans.-

Wright Town
Jabalpur (MP)

22 May 2015

Dear friend,
I am quite well here and hope for you to be hale and hearty there. As you know my birthday falls on 27 May. This year again, I am going to celebrate my birthday. I am giving a party on this occasion.
I invite to my birthday party.
Please do come. Your presence is most necessary.
My best regards to your parents.

Yours forever,


Vishal Ahuja

7. Write a letter to your friend telling him that you are unable to come to his birthday party.
Ans.

Adarsh Nagar
Satna (MP)

22 May 2015

Dear friend,
You needn't have told me about your birthday celebration through your letter. I know your birthday and you know I always come to you on your birthday.
But this time I can only wish you happy birthday through this letter. I have got a call letter from Maruti Udyog Limited. The date of interview falls exactly on 27 May 2015.
So I wish you many many happy returns of the day. I shall not be able to come to you this time but sure next time.
My best regards to your parents.
I am sending a watch for you as your birthday gift with this letter.

Yours sincerely,


Manoj Sharma

8.  Write a letter to your friend thanking him for the gift he sent you on your birthday.
    Ans.-

Wright Town
Jabalpur (MP)

28 May 2015

Dear friend,

I thank you for your gift that you sent for me. It is really a very beautiful and costly watch. My guests came on my birthday and I celebrated it with great pomp and show. But I always missed you. I kept on praying to God to give you success in your interview. My parents also wished you the same.
Do visit Jabalpur after the interview.
My best regards to your parents.

With warm regards,


Vishal Ahuja

9. Write a letter to your father telling him about your studies.
Ans.-

St. Mary's Hostel
St. John Convent School Indore

28 May 2015

Dear Daddy,
I am quite well here and hope that this letter of mine finds you in the best of your health and in a cheerful mood.
I got your letter yesterday. It seems that you are worried about my future. Daddy, I assure you that I won't waste even a single minute of my life. I am working hard. The result of the half yearly examination is open. I have stood first in it. I am trying to get a place in the top ten MP toppers.
I am sure that I will not fail in my ambition. The only thing that I need is blessings from you and mom.
Love to Mom and Pinky.

Yours affectionately,


Dheeraj Sharma

10. Write a letter to your father telling him what you want
to do after your Higher Secondary.
Ans.-

St. Mary's Hostel
Global Academy Jabalpur

28 May 2015

Dear father,
I am quite well here and hope that this letter of mine
finds you hale and hearty.
I got your letter yesterday. You advised me to prepare
for I.A.S. while doing B.S.C.
But I have thought of a different approach to success. I
am preparing for the I.I.T Entrance Examination J.E.E. I
am sure that I will get success in it.
Presently I.A.S. has lost its charm due to dirty politics.
I like research work better. It is a peaceful job. After my
B. Tech. I will try to take admission in MTech. It will
lead me towards research work. I feel that it is better
than I.A.S.
The rest is OK.
Love to Mom and Bunty.

Your loving son,


Jitendra Singh

11. Write a letter to your friend telling him what you want
to do after your Higher Secondary.

Ans.-

Adarsh Nagar
Satna (MP)

28 May 2018

Dear friend,
I am quite well here and hope that you are hale and hearty there.
I got your letter yesterday. I am happy to know that you are preparing for J.E.E.
I wish you great success in your attempt. But as you know I am a biology student, I will try for NEET. For the preparation of NEET, I shall not be a dropper for B.Sc. I will continue with my B.Sc. If I do not get success in NEET, I will go in for M.Sc. and then the research work.
The rest is OK. When are you coming to Satna?
Convey my best regards to your parents.

Warm regards,


Raviraj Sharma

12. Write a letter to your friend describing your visit to the Taj mahal.
Ans.-

Adarsh Nagar
Satna (MP)

28 May 2015

Dear friend,

I am quite well here and hope for the same to you. I am writing to you after a month because I had gone on a visit to the Taj. Really, it is really a wonderful experience.

It is really a very good experience to see the Taj. Its appearance is no doubt very attractive. It is more beautiful than what we see in pictures. Seeing the Taj face to face is a different experience. It is in fact a tomb. It was built by Shah-e-Jehan in the memory of beloved wife Mumtaz Mahal.

It is made entirely of white marble. It is built on a square platform having four minarets on its four corners. It has a big dome at the center. It appears the same from all the four sides. It is situated on the bank of the Yamuna. Seeing it in the moonlight is also a different experience.

If you go to Agra you must see it.

The rest is OK.

Convey my best regards to your parents.


Yours sincerely,


Ashish Singh

13. Write a letter to your friend consoling him on his failure in the examination.

Ans.-

Adarsh Nagar

Satna (MP)


28 May 2015


Dear friend,

I am sorry to know that you could not get success in the NEET examination and that you were very disappointed after your result. I came to know about it when my father was having a telephonic conversation with your father.

First of all, let me tell you that I could not believe my ears when I heard that you were depressed and disappointed. I thought you had nerves of steel. You always preached to me how to be strong and face the world and you yourself are showing that weakness. There is no doubt that reservation in educational institutions has worsened our fight and we have to put in our best of best efforts but if we blame it all on reservation, we shall be only complainers and whiners. Therefore, we must stop this blaming and complaining business. It will make you weak. You know it very well, failures are actually pillars of success. Failure only tells you that you did not put in sufficient effort and you have to change your strategy. Just think of Abraham Lincoln who kept failing all his life and when he succeeded, he became the President of America. Just don't be disheartened. Luck is also a factor that affects us but you will never be in bad luck all the time. One day good luck will follow you also.

Have patience and begin your fight again. I pray to God to give you success.

I want you to see a doctor. It will be greatly helpful to you to come out of depression.

Convey my best regards to your parents.

Waiting for good news.

Yours sincerely,


Rajkumar Mishra

14. Write a letter of condolence to your friend on the death of his mother.
Ans.-

Adarsh Nagar
Satna (MP)

28 May 2015

Dear friend,
I have no words to express how deeply I feel sorry at the sudden and tragic demise of your mother. I am so shocked to hear this news. I pray to God to give you strength to bear this irreparable loss. But it is only at the hands of God. We are merely puppets at the hands of God. You and your father did your best in the treatment of your mother but sometimes doctors too are helpless.
You must know dear friend that it is your father who really needs your support at this time. Be brave and don't let your father lose heart. I am always with you. I am coming to Jabalpur to be with you at this hour.
Now concentrate on your duties at present and don't think of past.

I shall be with you very soon.

Yours sincerely,


Shailendra Mishra

15. Write a letter to your friend telling him how to use the internet for improving your knowledge and get support for his studies.
Ans.-

Adarsh Nagar
Satna (MP)

28 May 2018

Dear friend,
I got your letter yesterday. I am happy that you trust me and discuss your problems with me. I am sorry to know that even after taking coaching of various subjects, you are performing poorly in all the subjects and you have not been able to improve your English.

Dear friend, you are a millionaire and you can spend money and get all the facilities. But I must tell you that unless you have a drive for learning, you will never learn. What is required is that you must be hungry to learn. Don't study just for passing the examination. Study with a view to knowing new things. If you have such a drive in you, your smart phone that I am sure you must be using in useless activities like chatting, facebook browsing and watching dirty video, can teach you everything that you need. Please pardon me for saying so but it is necessary.

Remember that the internet is the ocean of knowledge and it has everything that you need. It has educational information and relevant videos on all the subjects for all age group people. You can use this information and improve your knowledge on various subjects.

But I must warn you that there are several distractions on the internet that can make you go astray. You know very well that the internet has porn videos/apps and some dance video apps. Stop watching them if you are doing so. These videos will make you psychologically ill.

Remember, Facebook too is a great time waster. Facebook is only a social activity. You must limit its time. Concentrate on your curiosity to know the things, especially the items that are a part of your curriculum.

I am sure that you will heed to my advice and be benefitted.

Warm regards,


Manish Agrawal

**100 sentences useful for writing an informal letter.**
1.      I hope this letter finds you well.
2.      It's been too long since we last spoke.
3.      I'm writing to catch up with you.
4.      Thank you so much for your recent letter.
5.      I wanted to tell you about my recent trip.
6.      How have you been since we last met?
7.      I wanted to share some exciting news with you.
8.      I just wanted to drop you a quick line.
9.      I'm writing to invite you to my birthday party.
10.     I hope you're enjoying the summer/winter.
11.     I'm writing to ask for your advice on something.
12.     I've been thinking about you and wanted to reach out.
13.     I wanted to let you know how much I appreciate you.
14.     Remember when we used to...?
15.     It's been ages since we hung out together.
16.     I wanted to apologize for what happened the other day.
17.     I just had to write to tell you about this funny thing that happened.
18.     I'm writing to share my condolences for your loss.
19.     I can't wait to see you next week!
20.     I'm so sorry to hear about what happened.
21.     Congratulations on your recent achievement!

22.     I'm writing to tell you about a great book I just read.

23.     Thank you for being such a great friend.

24.     I wanted to let you know how much your support means to me.

25.     How's everything going with your new job?

26.     I've been meaning to write to you for ages.

27.     I'm writing to check in on you and see how you're doing.

28.     I hope you're not too busy to read this letter.

29.     I wanted to share some updates about my life.

30.     Let's plan a get-together soon!

31.     I'm writing to invite you to come visit me.

32.     I'm really looking forward to seeing you soon.

33.     I hope you can make it to the party next weekend.

34.     I just wanted to say a quick hello.

35.     I've been thinking about the fun times we had together.

36.     I'm writing to tell you about my new hobby.

37.     It's been too quiet around here without you.

38.     I miss our long chats over coffee.

39.     I wanted to let you know I'll be in town next month.

40.     I'm writing to share some good news with you.

41.     How's your family doing?

42.     I wanted to thank you for your kindness.

43.     I hope you had a wonderful holiday season.

44.     I'm writing to ask for your help with something.

45.     I've been feeling a bit down lately and thought writing to you might help.

46.     I'm writing to invite you to be part of a special event.

47.     I'm writing to tell you about a funny dream I had last night.

48.     I can't believe how quickly time is flying by!

49.     I wanted to let you know how much I admire you.
50.     I'm writing to apologize for not keeping in touch more often.
51.     I hope you're enjoying your new home/job.
52.     I wanted to share some photos from my recent trip with you.
53.     I've been reminiscing about our school days lately.
54.     I'm writing to let you know about a great restaurant I discovered.
55.     I hope we can catch up soon over a cup of coffee.
56.     I'm writing to invite you to join me for a hike next weekend.
57.     I wanted to tell you about this hilarious movie I watched.
58.     I hope this letter brings a smile to your face.
59.     I'm writing to express my gratitude for everything you've done for me.
60.     I wanted to share my thoughts on a recent news article with you.
61.     I hope you're taking care of yourself.
62.     I'm writing to let you know I'll be thinking of you.
63.     I just wanted to say how much I appreciate our friendship.
64.     I'm writing to tell you about the crazy weather we've been having.
65.     I wanted to thank you for always being there for me.
66.     I'm so excited to hear about your upcoming plans.
67.     I hope you're finding time to relax and unwind.
68.     I'm writing to ask if you'd like to go to the concert with me.
69.     I wanted to share some exciting updates about my life with you.

70.    I hope you're enjoying your weekend.
71.    I'm writing to share a funny story about my pets.
72.    I wanted to tell you about this amazing book I just finished reading.
73.    I hope you can make it to my graduation ceremony.
74.    I'm writing to let you know I'll be thinking of you on your birthday.
75.    I'm sorry for not keeping in touch more regularly.
76.    I wanted to share some advice with you.
77.    I hope this letter finds you in good health and spirits.
78.    I'm writing to invite you to my housewarming party.
79.    I wanted to let you know I'm here for you if you need anything.
80.    I'm writing to share some exciting news about my job.
81.    I hope we can meet up for lunch soon.
82.    I'm writing to ask if you'd like to go on a road trip together.
83.    I wanted to share my thoughts on a recent movie I watched.
84.    I hope you're enjoying your summer vacation.
85.    I'm writing to tell you about my latest DIY project.
86.    I wanted to let you know I'm thinking of you during this difficult time.
87.    I'm so grateful to have you as a friend.
88.    I hope we can plan a beach day together soon.
89.    I'm writing to invite you to my holiday party.
90.    I wanted to share some delicious recipes I've been trying out.
91.    I hope you're staying safe and healthy.
92.    I'm writing to share some updates about my family with you.

93.    I wanted to let you know how much your friendship means to me.

94.    I'm writing to ask if you'd like to go camping with me this summer.

95.    I hope you're enjoying your new hobby.

96.    I wanted to share some funny anecdotes from work with you.

97.    I'm writing to invite you to join me for a weekend getaway.

98.    I hope this letter brings some joy to your day.

99.    I wanted to tell you about the amazing concert I went to last night.

100.    I'm looking forward to hearing from you soon.

***

**Congratulatory Messages**

1.    Congratulations on your new job!

2.    Well done on your recent promotion.

3.    Wishing you all the best in your new home.

4.    Congratulations on your engagement!

5.    I'm so happy for you on your graduation.

6.    Best wishes on your retirement.

7.    Congratulations on the birth of your baby.

8.    You did an amazing job, congratulations!

9.    I'm thrilled to hear about your success.

10.    Congratulations on your anniversary!

**Condolences**

1.    I am deeply sorry for your loss.

2.    My thoughts and prayers are with you during this difficult time.

3.    Please accept my heartfelt condolences.

4.    I am here for you if you need anything.

5.    Wishing you peace and comfort during this tough time.

6.    My deepest sympathies go out to you and your family.

7.    May the memories of (Name) bring you comfort.

8.    I am so sorry to hear about your loss.

9.      You are in my thoughts and prayers.
10.     May you find strength in the love and support of friends and family.

**Apologies**

1.      I apologize for any inconvenience I may have caused.
2.      I am truly sorry for my actions.
3.      Please accept my sincerest apologies.
4.      I regret any hurt my words may have caused.
5.      I am sorry and I will ensure it doesn't happen again.
6.      I hope you can forgive me for my mistake.
7.      I apologize for the misunderstanding.
8.      I am sorry for any trouble I may have caused.
9.      Please accept my apology and know that I value our relationship.
10.     I am deeply sorry for any distress I may have caused you.

**Opening Statements**

1.      I hope this email finds you well.
2.      I am writing to you regarding (subject).
3.      I am writing to follow up on our previous conversation.
4.      I hope you are having a productive week.
5.      I wanted to reach out to discuss (topic).
6.      I am writing to inform you about (update).
7.      I hope you are doing well.
8.      I wanted to touch base with you about (subject).
9.      I am writing to request (information/action).
10.     I hope you had a great weekend.

### Exercise – 1.

1. Write a letter to your friend telling him/her the advantages and disadvantages of social media.

2. Write a letter to your father requesting him to send you money to buy a smart-phone giving valid reasons how it will help you.
3. Write a letter to your father inquiring about the health of your mother.
4. Write a letter to your younger brother who lives in a hostel telling him the importance of early rising.
5. Write a letter to your friend telling him/her the advantages of reading English newspapers and magazines.
6. Write a letter to your friend who could not get admission in a medical college even after working hard for three years and taking support of a famous coaching center.
7. Write a letter of condolence to your friend whose father has died in a car accident.
8. Write a letter to your younger brother advising him how to handle antisocial elements and how to avoid the company of bad boys.
9. Write a letter to your father about unhealthy living conditions and poor quality of food in the hostel you are living in.
10. Write a letter to your friend requesting him/her to help you in getting a job in the organization where he/she is working.

# Part 3

# *Kinds of Formal Letters*

*This
Part
Contains
Classification
Of
Formal Letters
Or
Kinds
Of
Formal Letters*

# Formal Letters

There are a number of formal letters that are written in our formal life. We can broadly divide them into four categories

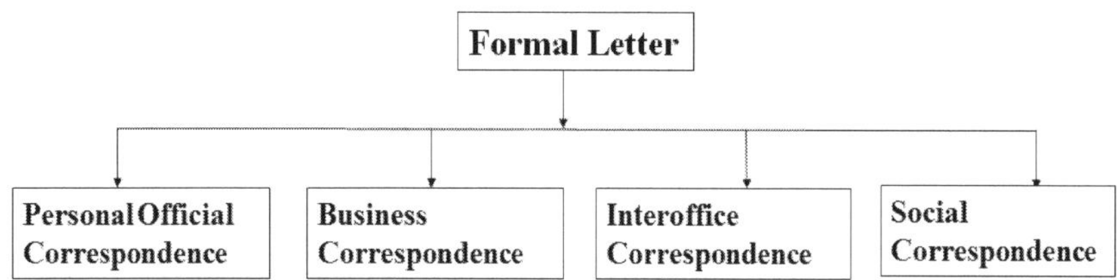



## Personal Official Correspondence

It is your personal formal correspondence with any office or any organization e.g. application to the principal, application/letter to the collector or any other head of the department of government or private organization or application letter for job etc.(Remember that the letters that you write on behalf of an organization as its employee do not come under this category). It stands out from the rest by the fact that the receiver end of this letter is official and the sender end is personal that is why the name Personal Official Correspondence has been assigned to it.

## Business Correspondence

It is the correspondence that a business organization enters into with another organization. It may be relating to all sorts of business activities or the activities relating to smooth functioning of an organization e.g. sales letter, letter of quotation/enquiry, placing the order, letter of complaint and credit and collection letter and correspondence with any government organization etc.

## Inter office correspondence

This is the correspondence that takes place between two offices of the same organization or between the people of the same organization on official matters. Inter-office memos and reports can be included in this category.

## Social Correspondence

Man is a social animal. Socializing is an important activity for amicable relations with people in the society. We have to write invitations to dinner, birthday parties, etc. These invitations or their replies or condolence messages / letters can be included in social correspondence.

# Part 4

# *Applications to the Principal*

*This
Part
Contains
Different
Types
Of Applications/letters
To The Principal
Or
To The Head of
An Educational
Institutions*

# Personal Official Correspondence

Possibly the first formal letter you might have written is the letter/application to the principal of your school.

# Application to the Principal

**Lay out of an application to the principal**

An application to the Principal is written on a different layout.

The following figure will help you know what to write and where. You can see the layout on the next page.

(1.Inside Address e.g.)
The Principal
SHS School
Nirala Nagar Rewa (MP)

(2.Salutation e.g.)
 Respected Sir,

(3.Subject)

(4. Main Body of the letter)
...........................................................................................................
...........................................................................................................
...........................................................................................................
...........................................................................................................
...........................................................................................................
...........................................................................................................
...........................................................................................................
...........................................................................................................
...................................................................................

(5.Complimentary  close)

(7. Place)
(8. Date)

(6.Signature)

**1. Inside Address-**Inside Address is the address of the receiver of the letter/application.

Write at place no.1:-

The Principal

The Address of the School/College

( You can write "To The Principal" also however 'To' is not necessary because  this place is meant for the receiver of the application. But remember that "P" must be capital when you write "The Principal".)

   Write the address of the school or college under "The Principal".

## 7. *Salutation-Write "Respected Sir" Or "Sir" at place no 2.*

## 8. *Subject- It should be as brief as possible.*

**4. Main Body-**You may start the main body of application in the following manner: -

 I beg to say that.............

Or

I beg to state that................

Or

Sir,

   Most respectfully I beg to say that.................

Or

You may come directly on the point

**5. Complimentary Close-** You may write "Yours faithfully" or "Yours obediently" for complimentary close of the application at place no 6.

**6. Signature-** Put down your signature under complimentary close and then write your name.

**7+ 8-** Besides this, on the left margin, you should write the date (Always spell the name of the month) and the name of the place from where you are writing the letter/application.

***

# 'Subject' should come after 'salutation' or before 'salutation'?

(See figure for better understanding) People generally write 'subject line 'before 'salutation' but you can see letters having 'subject line' after salutation also. It is quite natural to have a question in your mind which convention is right.

Here I would like to say that both the conventions are right but however, I would like to add that using the subject line after salutation is better because greeting precedes all communication.

***

<u>**Specimen Application to the Principal**</u>

The Principal
JP Institute of Technology
Chhatarpur  Road Sagar (MP)

Sir

Subject-Application for the membership of ISTE

Most respectfully, I beg to say that I want to become a member of ISTE. I am Rupesh Ahuja from Electrical Engineering $6^{th}$ Semester. I have come to know from our professors that all the faculty members have become members of ISTE. Students too can become members of this society. This society publishes a magazine and there are various advantages that we can get from it.

I request you to permit me to become a member of ISTE and provide necessary support.

I am ready to pay the subscription there of.

Thank you,

Yours faithfully

Rupesh Ahuja


Place- Sagar

Date- 12 July,2005

***

# Sample Applications to the Principal of an Educational Institution

1. Write an application to the Principal of your school requesting him to grant you leave on medical background.
   Ans.-

   The Principal
   Saraswati Higher Secondary School
   Krishna Nagar Sagar (MP)

   Respected Sir,

   Subject: Leave on account of illness.

   I beg to say that I have been suffering from fever since last night. The doctor has advised me to take a complete rest for three days.
   Therefore, I request you to grant me leave for three days i.e. from 16 July 2015 to 18 July 2015 and oblige.
   Thank you.

   Yours faithfully,


   Ravi
   Place- Sagar (MP)
   Date- 17 July 2015
2. Write an application to the Principal of your school requesting him to grant you leave on account of your brother's marriage.
   Ans.-

The Principal
Saraswati Higher Secondary School
Krishna Nagar Sagar (MP)

Respected Sir,

Subject: Leave on account of brother's marriage.

I beg to say that my brother is going to be married on 29 November 2015. I shall have to be at home during the marriage. I shall be busy for a week.

Therefore, I request you to grant me leave for a week i.e. from 16 July 2015 to 24 July 2015 and oblige.
Thank you.

Yours faithfully,

Ravi Sharma
Place- Sagar (MP)
Date- 17 July 2015

3. Write an application to the Principal of your school for a transfer certificate.
   Ans.-

The Principal
Saraswati Higher Secondary School
Krishna Nagar Satna (MP)

Respected Sir,

Subject: Transfer certificate.

I beg to say that I am a student of class X- (C) of your school. My father has been transferred to Bhopal so it is not possible for me to study here.

Therefore, I request you to issue me a transfer certificate and oblige.
Thank you.

Yours faithfully,

Rajesh
Place- Sagar (MP)
Date- 17 July 2015

4. Write an application to the Principal of your school for a full free ship.
Ans.-

The Principal
Sindhu Higher Secondary School
Sagar Road Banda (MP)

Respected Sir,

Subject: Full free ship.

I beg to say that I am a student of class X- (C) of your school. I am a poor student. My father is a teacher in a private school. His salary is Rs 5000 per month. This amount is hardly enough for us to make our both ends meet.
Therefore, I request you to grant me full free ship and oblige.
Thank you.

Yours faithfully,


Mahesh
Place- Banda (MP)
Date- 17 July 2015

5.  Write an application to the Principal of your school for a scholarship.
Ans.-

The Principal
Sindhu Higher Secondary School
Sagar Road Banda (MP)

Respected Sir,

Subject: Scholarship.

I am a student of class X  (C) of your school.
I beg to apply for scholarship on the following grounds: -
  (i)        I have been getting the scholarship for the last three years.
  (ii)       I stood first in my class last year.
  (iii)      I am the Captain of my school handball team.
  (iv)       I have won the Inter School Handball Championship three times.
I am sure that in the light of above qualifications you will grant me scholarship and oblige.
Thank you.

Yours faithfully,


Sankalp Mishra
Place- Banda (MP)
Date- 17 July 2015

6.  Write an application to the Principal of your school requesting him to issue books from the book bank.
Ans.-

The Principal

Saraswati Higher Secondary School
Krishna Nagar Sagar (MP)

Respected Sir,

Subject: Books from book bank.

I beg to say that I am a poor student of class X (B) of your school. My father is a teacher in a private school. He gets a very low salary.
So it is not possible for me to buy all the books from the market.
Therefore I request you to issue me books from the book bank and oblige.
Thank you.

Yours faithfully,


Manish Singh
Place- Sagar (MP)
Date- 17 July 2015

7. Write an application to the Principal of your school for the permission of going on a tour.
   Ans.-

   The Principal
   Saraswati Higher Secondary School
   Krishna Nagar Sagar (MP)

   Respected Sir,

   Subject: Permission for a tour.

I beg to say that I am the Monitor of class XI- (A). The students of my class want to go on a tour to Agra and Mathura in the holidays of Deepawali.

Therefore I request you to permit us to go on this tour.

Besides this, I also request you to make necessary arrangements for this tour like deciding fees and sending some teachers also with us to maintain discipline in the tour.

Thank you.

Yours faithfully,

Ravendra Jain
Place- Sagar (MP)
Date- 17 July 2015

8. Write an application to the Principal of your school to permit your team to play a friendly match in the school playground.
   Ans.-

The Principal
T.M.A. Higher Secondary School
Rewa Road Satna (MP)

Respected Sir,

Subject: Permission for a friendly cricket match.

I beg to say that I am the Captain of my school cricket team. The team of Saraswati H.S. School wants to play a friendly cricket match with us in our school playground.

Kindly grant us permission to play this match on our school playground tomorrow i.e. 27 July 2015 from 10 AM.

Please arrange for some teachers also to maintain discipline in the playground.
Thank you.

Yours faithfully,


Shanu Goyal
Place- Satna (MP)
Date- 17 July 2015

9. Write an application to the Principal of your school requesting him to change your subject.
Ans.-

The Principal
Subhash Higher Secondary School
Rewa road Satna (MP)

Respected Sir,

Subject: Change of the subjects.

I beg to say that I am a student of class XI- (A) of your school. I offered Special English as one of my subjects. But now I find that it is very difficult for me to carry on with this subject. I cannot do well in this subject.
I want to take General English in place of Special English.
Therefore I request you to change my subjects and oblige.
Thank you.


Yours faithfully,


Mahendra Singh

Place- Satna (MP)
Date- 17 July 2015

10. Write an application to the Principal of your school requesting him to issue a character certificate for you.
Ans.-

The Principal
Saraswati Higher Secondary School
Krishna Nagar Rewa (MP)

Respected Sir,

Subject: Character Certificate.

I beg to say that I am a poor student of class X- (B) of your school. I have passed class X in the first division. I want to take admission in Rewa Polytechnic College. I need a character certificate with TC in this regard.
Please issue me a C.C. with T.C.
Thank you.

Yours faithfully,


Manoj Tiwari
Place- Rewa (MP)
Date- 17 July 2015

11. Write an application to the Principal of your school requesting him to change the timing of the bus.
Ans.-

The Principal
Subhash Higher Secondary School
Rewa Road Satna (MP)

Respected Sir,

Subject: Request to change the timing of the bus

I regret to bring it to your kind consideration that all the girls of the commerce section including me that go by bus have to idle about for at least two hours without any work every day. After the second recess, (3PM) all the girls that go by the bus do not have any lectures. They idle about here and there or gossip with their friends. The bus comes at 5PM. Thus, two precious hours of ours are wasted daily. Our parents too are against remaining in the school without any engagement.
I request you to change the timing of the bus and make it 3.15 PM and oblige.
Thank you.


Yours faithfully,


Dharmendra Singh
Place- Satna (MP)
Date- 17 July 2015

12. You are Manish Sharma, a student of class X in Saraswati Higher Secondary School Rajendra Nagar Satna. The bus stop of your school bus is one kilometer from your locality although there are a sufficient number of students from your locality. Write an application to the Principal of your school requesting him to shift the bus stop to your locality.
Ans.-

The Principal
Saraswati Higher Secondary School
Rajendra Nagar Satna (MP)

Respected Sir,

Subject: Regarding shifting the bus stop.

I beg to say that I am a student of class X (B) in your school. I board the school bus from Dhawari square near the stadium. I come from street number one which is one kilometer from Dhawari square. There are eleven other students like me. We have to walk one kilometer to catch the bus every day although the bus can be sent to our locality i.e. street number one also. No student boards from Dhawari square except us.
Therefore, I request you to shift the stop of the school bus from Dhawari square to street number one Dhawari and oblige.
Thank you.

Yours faithfully,


Manish Sharma
Place- Satna (MP)
Date- 17 July 2015
**Useful and Important Sentences for Application to the Principal (school)**
1.      I am writing to request permission to participate in the upcoming school trip.
2.      I would like to apply for the position of (position name) in the student council.
3.      I am writing to request a meeting with you to discuss an important matter.
4.      I am seeking approval to organize a charity event in collaboration with our school.
5.      I would like to request an extension for submitting my assignment due to (reason).

6.      I am writing to request your permission to conduct a science experiment in the laboratory.
7.      I am applying for a scholarship to support my further studies.
8.      I am writing to seek your approval for organizing a cultural event in our school.
9.      I am requesting leave from school due to illness.
10.     I am writing to express my interest in joining the school's debate club.
11.     I would like to request a copy of my academic transcripts for college applications.
12.     I am applying for the position of library monitor in our school.
13.     I am writing to request your assistance in resolving a conflict with another student.
14.     I am seeking your permission to organize a field trip for our class.
15.     I am writing to request a recommendation letter from you for my college application.
16.     I am applying for the role of class representative for the upcoming academic year.
17.     I am requesting your permission to use the school auditorium for a drama performance.
18.     I am writing to request additional study materials for my upcoming exams.
19.     I am applying for a part-time job in the school library.
20.     I am seeking your approval to start a new club focused on environmental awareness.
21.     I am writing to request a change in my elective subject due to personal reasons.
22.     I am applying for a leave of absence from school to attend a family function.
23.     I am requesting your support in organizing a sports tournament in our school.
24.     I am writing to seek your advice on choosing the right career path.

25.    I would like to request your assistance in resolving a scheduling conflict with my classes.
26.    I am applying for permission to conduct a survey among students for my project.
27.    I am writing to request your guidance on improving the facilities in our school library.
28.    I am seeking approval for a fundraising event to support a local charity.
29.    I am applying for an internship opportunity with a local organization and need your recommendation.
30.    I am writing to request a school leaving certificate as I am transferring to another school.
31.    I am seeking permission to organize a cleanliness drive in our school campus.
32.    I am writing to request your support for organizing an educational workshop for students.
33.    I am applying for a scholarship to attend a summer program in (subject).
34.    I am requesting your approval to start a new extracurricular club focusing on robotics.
35.    I am writing to seek your permission to conduct a survey on student satisfaction with cafeteria food.
36.    I am applying for the position of sports captain for the upcoming sports season.
37.    I am seeking your assistance in resolving an issue regarding the school bus transportation service.
38.    I am writing to request your permission to host a career guidance seminar for students.
39.    I am applying for a spot on the school's basketball team.
40.    I am seeking your approval to organize a blood donation camp in our school.
41.    I am writing to request your support in organizing a science fair for students.
42.    I am applying for a scholarship to attend a leadership conference.

43.     I am seeking permission to organize a talent show for students.
44.     I am writing to request your guidance on preparing for college entrance exams.
45.     I am applying for a spot in the school's drama club.
46.     I am seeking your approval for a new recycling initiative in our school.
47.     I am writing to request your assistance in resolving a bullying issue I am facing.
48.     I am applying for permission to start a peer tutoring program in our school.
49.     I am seeking your approval to organize a guest lecture by a renowned speaker.
50.     I am writing to request your support in organizing a community service project for students.
51.     I am writing to request an extension for submitting my research paper due to (reason).
52.     I am applying for an internship opportunity with (company name) and need your approval.
53.     I would like to request your assistance in obtaining access to specialized software for my project.
54.     I am seeking permission to organize a career fair on campus.
55.     I am writing to request your support in organizing a seminar on (topic).
56.     I am applying for a leave of absence from college due to personal reasons.
57.     I am seeking your guidance on applying for study abroad programs.
58.     I am writing to request your approval for a study group to be formed in our department.
59.     I am applying for a scholarship to support my academic expenses.
60.     I am seeking permission to conduct a survey among students for my research project.

61.    I would like to request a change in my major/subject due to my evolving interests.
62.    I am writing to request a meeting with you to discuss academic concerns.
63.    I am applying for permission to organize a cultural event on campus.
64.    I am seeking your assistance in resolving a conflict with a faculty member.
65.    I am writing to request your support for organizing a sports tournament among college departments.
66.    I am applying for a grant to support a community service project I am involved in.
67.    I am seeking permission to use the college auditorium for a student-led performance.
68.    I am writing to request access to additional library resources for my thesis.
69.    I am applying for permission to start a new student club focused on entrepreneurship.
70.    I am seeking your approval to organize a workshop on academic writing skills.
71.    I am writing to request your assistance in resolving an issue regarding housing accommodations.
72.    I am applying for an academic award/recognition based on my performance.
73.    I am seeking your support in organizing an alumni networking event for students.
74.    I am writing to request your guidance on career planning and job search strategies.
75.    I am applying for a spot on the college's debate team.
76.    I am seeking your approval for a field trip for students in my department.
77.    I am writing to request your assistance in obtaining a letter of recommendation for graduate school.

78.     I am applying for permission to organize a fundraiser for a charitable cause.
79.     I am seeking permission to conduct a workshop on mental health awareness for students.
80.     I am writing to request your support in organizing a research symposium.
81.     I am applying for a scholarship to attend a conference relevant to my field of study.
82.     I am seeking your approval to start a mentorship program for freshmen students.
83.     I am writing to request your assistance in resolving an issue with course registration.
84.     I am applying for permission to organize a career development seminar for students.
85.     I am seeking your guidance on applying for summer research opportunities.
86.     I am writing to request access to additional lab equipment for my project.
87.     I am applying for a grant to support my participation in a national academic competition.
88.     I am seeking your approval to organize a series of guest lectures by industry experts.
89.     I am writing to request your support in obtaining an internship opportunity with (company name).
90.     I am applying for permission to organize an educational trip for students.
91.     I am seeking your assistance in resolving a financial aid issue I am facing.
92.     I am writing to request your approval for a study abroad program I am interested in.
93.     I am applying for permission to use college facilities for a student-led research conference.
94.     I am seeking your guidance on applying for graduate school programs.
95.     I am writing to request your support for organizing a campus-wide environmental sustainability campaign.

96.     I am applying for a leave of absence from college to pursue a short-term project.

97.     I am seeking your approval to start a volunteer program for students in the local community.

98.     I am writing to request your assistance in resolving a conflict within my student organization.

99.     I am applying for permission to organize a hackathon event on campus.

100.    I am seeking your support in obtaining funding for a student-initiated research project.

## Exercise-2.

1. Write an application to the Principal of your school/college requesting him/her to create a facility of book bank in the library so that students may get all the required books for the whole year.

2. Write an application to the Principal of your school/college requesting him/her to arrange for a lecture of spoken English as many students are very poor in English.

3. Write an application to the Principal of your school/college complaining against the rude behavior of the lab assistant in the Chemistry Lab.

4. Write an application to the Principal of your school/college complaining about the crowded school bus by which you come to college.

5. Write an application to the Principal of your school/college requesting him/her to give fee     concession because you are two brothers reading in the same school.

6. Write an application to the Principal of your school/college complaining against some antisocial elements that keep standing in front of the school gate and do the eve teasing when the girls leave the college.

7. Write an application to the Principle of your college/school requesting him/her to change the teacher of mathematics because he/she is not competent enough to teach students.

8.  Write an application to the Principal of your college / school requesting him/her to permit the publication of college/school magazine and make requisite arrangement for the same because many students in the school/college are interested in contributing to the magazine by their writings.

9.  Write an application to the Principal of your college / school requesting him/her to permit you to leave early for your home today because you have urgent work at home.

10. Write an application to the Principal of your college / school requesting him/her to arrange for some important newspapers and magazines in the college/school library.

# Part 5

## *Applications to the Collector or Head of any Public /Government Organization or Private Organization*

*This Part Contains Different Types of
Letters /Applications
To the Collector,
Head of any Government/
Private Organization
Or
The Editor of a Newspaper*

# Application to the Collector or The Head of any institution / government institution

Like an application to the Principal you can write any letter to the head of an institution. This is also a formal letter. The difference is that you have to write your address and date on the top right-hand corner and the remaining things are the same as we write in an application to the Principal. This type of letter may be an application, a complaint or an inquiry.

## Lay out of an application to the Collector or The Head of any institution / government institution

The following figure will help you know what to write and where.

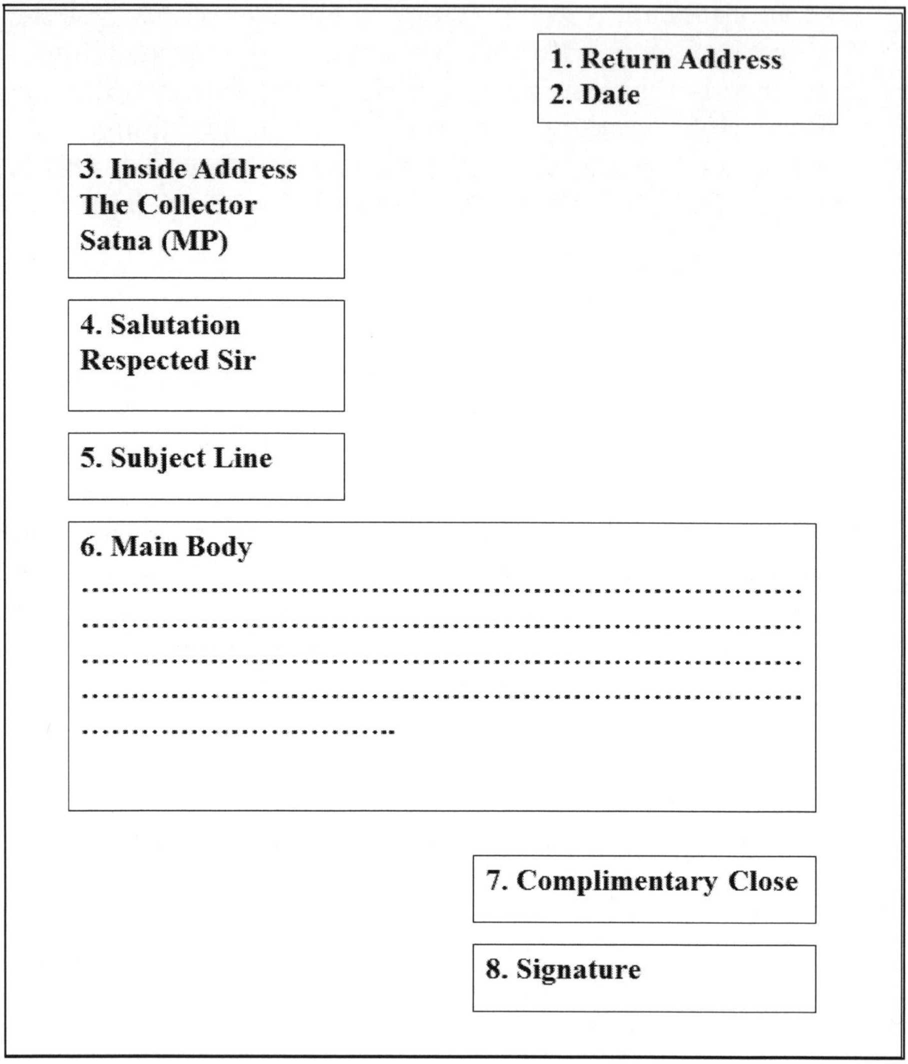

<table>
<tr><td></td><td align="right">1. Return Address<br>2. Date</td></tr>
<tr><td>3. Inside Address<br>The Collector<br>Satna (MP)</td><td></td></tr>
<tr><td>4. Salutation<br>Respected Sir</td><td></td></tr>
<tr><td>5. Subject Line</td><td></td></tr>
<tr><td colspan="2">6. Main Body<br>........................................................................................<br>........................................................................................<br>........................................................................................<br>........................................................................................<br>.....................................................</td></tr>
<tr><td></td><td>7. Complimentary Close</td></tr>
<tr><td></td><td>8. Signature</td></tr>
</table>

A sample letter of complaint to the Collector

Civil Lines Satna (MP)
23 Feb,2005

The Collector
Satna (MP)

Respected Sir,

Subject-Complaint against dangerous road conditions

I regret to bring to your notice that Satna Panna road in the Pateri area is extremely dangerous to travel.

This road has been laid recently and therefore it is a good temptation for rash drivers. But the sideways of the road are too deep in comparison to the road.

Many times, speeding four-wheelers force the two-wheelers to go on the sideways. But since the layers of the road have made the road too high, it is extremely dangerous to jump the vehicle upon the sideways. The road layers have raised the road but did not elevate the sideways properly.

Therefore I request you to take interest in the matter and instruct the concerned department to elevate the sideways properly so that any untoward incident may be avoided.

Thank you,

Yours faithfully,

Manish Sharma

# Some more letters written to the Head of any Organization

1. Write an application to the Collector of your District requesting him to ban the use of loudspeakers during your examination.
   Ans.

Krishna Nagar
Satna (MP)
17 July 2015

The Collector
Civil Lines Satna (MP)

Respected Sir,

Subject: Application to ban loudspeakers.

I regret to bring it to your kind consideration that loudspeakers in my locality are creating a great disturbance in our studies.

I am a student of class XII. Our examinations are going to start next week but since it is the time of marriages, people are playing film songs on the loudspeakers round the clock. Besides this, marriage processions use high volume loudspeakers. Besides being a nuisance to our studies, these loudspeakers are harmful to health also.

You know very well how precious our time is. We cannot do any reading because of these loudspeakers.

Therefore I request you to put a ban on the use of loudspeakers during our examination time and oblige.
Thank you.

Yours faithfully,

Rajesh Shukla

2. Write a letter of complaint against a careless postman of your area to the Head Postmaster of your city.
Ans.-

Bharhut Nagar
Satna (MP)
17 July 2015

The Head Postmaster
Head Post Office
Jaistambh Chowk Satna (MP)

Respected Sir,

Subject: Complaint against a postman.

I am sorry to bring it to your kind consideration that the postman of our area Nathuram is very negligent and dishonest.
He always delivers letters very late. He sometimes gives letters to wrong hands also. One day I got my personal letter already opened. People miss dinners, appointments, invitations and jobs due to his negligence.
Therefore I request you to take strong action against him and provide another postman for our area.
Thank you.

Yours faithfully,
Mahesh Varma


3. You are Sarita Das, a resident of Bajrang Nagar and a student of TRS college Rewa . Some antisocial elements

collected at Sirmour Chowk indulge in eve teasing whenever you pass by the squire. Your oral warning had no effect on them but it has worsened the situation. Their number is increasing day by day. The girls with you are also very much frightened. Write a letter to the Superintendent of Police Rewa requesting him to take appropriate action in this regard.
Ans.-

Bajrang Nagar
Rewa(MP)
19 July 2017

The Superintendent of Police
Rewa (MP)

Respected Sir,

Subject: Eve teasing by some antisocial elements at Sirmour Squire.

I am a resident of Bajrang Nagar and a college going girl BSC first year TRS college Rewa. There are a total of five girls in my group. We come to Sirmour Chowk or foot from our homes in Bajrang Nagar and we take the auto from Sirmour Chowk for our college. A group of some antisocial elements is always present here before our arrival and they pass dirty comments on us and sing film songs. We first of all ignored it but they became even more daring. I warned them orally but they appear to be hardcore hoodlums and it had no effect on them. Another problem is that their number is on the increase. None of us has informed our family members about it for fear that it may lead to physical confrontation between our family members and these elements..

I request you to take appropriate action against these elements before things take an ugly turn.

Thank you very much.

Yours faithfully,


Sarita Das


4.  You are Manish Sharma a resident of Adarsh Nagar Rewa. There is an open ground before your house meant for a stadium but the construction of the stadium has yet to be started. A tractor trolley comes to the ground daily and dumps the garbage of the city here. You complained to concerned people but it had no effect. Write a letter to the Commissioner Municipal Corporation Rewa requesting him to take appropriate action in this regard.
Ans.-

Adarsh Nagar
Rewa (MP)
19 July 2017

The Commissioner
Municipal Corporation
Rewa (MP)

Respected Sir,

Subject: Garbage dumping in the proposed stadium.

I am Manish Sharma, a resident of Adarsh Nagar Rewa. There is an open ground in front of my house. It is meant for a stadium as is proposed by the Municipal Corporation. The construction of the stadium has yet not started and we don't know when it will start. However the municipal corporation has converted it into a dumping yard for the garbage of the whole city. A tractor trolley comes to the ground daily and dumps the garbage of the city here. It has become a mountain of garbage. It has started giving off a stinking smell. Now there is a great danger of outbreak of epidemics unless quick action is taken. We were opposed to it in the beginning but the driver of the tractor trolley said that he would do what he had been instructed. We informed our ward member about it but he too is not able to give us a satisfactory explanation.

I request you to intervene in the matter and take appropriate action against those who took the decision to dump garbage here. I also request you to remove all the garbage from here before the rains start otherwise exposure to a dirty environment may cause serious ailments.

Thank you very much.

Yours faithfully,


Manish Sharma


5. You are Abhishek Sharma Kothi No1 Morar Gwalior. Write an application to the Municipal Commissioner complaining about insanitary conditions of your locality.

Ans.-

Kothi No1 Morar
Gwalior (MP)
17 July 2015

The Municipal Commissioner
Municipal Corporation
Fort Road Gwalior (MP)

Respected Sir,

Subject: Complaint against insanitary conditions.

I regret to inform you that there is a great danger of epidemics in my locality Morar due to insanitary conditions prevailing here.

A mound of dirt and garbage which has been collected here in the Gandhi Park has not been removed for 14 months. On the contrary, a tractor trolley is still dumping dirt and garbage in it. After the rainy season it has begun to give a stinking smell and it is impossible for people of this locality to live here. There is a great danger of epidemics in the locality.

Therefore, I request you to get the area cleaned and oblige all the people here.

Thank you.

Yours faithfully,


Abhishek Sharma

6. You are Abhishek Tiwari, Street No 9 Rajendra Nagar Satna (MP). Write an application to the Secretary MP Board of Secondary Education Bhopal (MP) for a duplicate mark sheet.

Ans.-

Street No 9
Rajendra Nagar Satna (MP)
17 July 2015

The Secretary
MP Board of Education
Bhopal (MP)

Respected Sir,

Subject: Application for a duplicate marksheet.

I beg to say that I am a student of class XI in Saraswati Higher Secondary School Satna (MP) . I appeared in the High School Certificate Examination last year and passed in the first division. My Roll No was 46879756.
But unfortunately, I have lost my mark sheet.
I request you to send me a duplicate mark sheet.
I am sending a DD of Rs 200 with this application as fee to the mark sheet.
Thank you.

Yours faithfully,


Abhishek Tiwari

7. You are Rachana Shrivastava, a student of class XII in Nehru Public School Rewa. You go to school on foot because your school is near your house. But you find some antisocial elements on your way. Write a letter of complaint to the S.P. of your District.
Ans.-

Adarsh Nagar Rewa
17 July 2015

The Superintendent of Police
Rewa (MP)

Respected Sir,

Subject: Complaint against antisocial element.

I am a student (Rachana Shrivastava) of Nehru Public School Rewa. I live near my school. I have to walk 300 meters to reach my school.
But almost every day, I come across some antisocial elements in my street. They keep standing beside a pan shop and cut lewd remarks on the girls going to school.
I request you to arrange for some police patrolmen when the school opens and closes.
Thank you.

Yours faithfully,


Rachana Shrivastava


8. You are Ravi Verma Krishna Nagar Allahabad. Write a letter of complaint against a bus conductor of UPSRTC Lucknow.
Ans.-

Krishna Nagar Allahabad
17 July 2015

The Manager UPSRTC
Lucknow (UP)

Respected Sir,

Subject: Complaint against a bus conductor.

I regret to inform you that the bus conductor on board Allahabad Lucknow bus that leaves from Allahabad for Lucknow at 9AM by not returning the balance.

I boarded the bus when it was leaving. He took a one thousand rupee note from me and gave me the ticket. When I asked for the balance, he said that the bus was crowded and I would get the balance at Lucknow.

But when I reached Lucknow, the conductor got down and disappeared. I waited for him in the bus stand for a very long time but he did not appear. I asked the bus driver about him, but he too was helpless. I left my address and phone no with the booking clerk for further developments and left for the office where I had important work. Even after a month, I have not got the balance amount. On another occasion, I visited the Lucknow office and I met the bus conductor. But he refused to pay the balance amount because he said he did not owe it and that he had paid the entire balance amount.

Now I request you to take strong action against such a dishonest bus conductor so that it may be a lesson for others.

Thank you.


Yours faithfully,


Ravi Verma

9. You are Rakesh Ravi from Wright Town Jabalpur. You are pained to read in the newspaper how people become victims of dhongi babas specially minor girls who are raped by these dhongi babas in their ashrams. These girls become victims because of the superstitions of their parents because they are sent to the ashrams of these babajis by their parents. Parents think that their

daughter will become virtuous or they will be cured of their illness. Write a letter to the Editor of a local newspaper expressing your concern. [dhongi (from Hindi)= fake, hypocrite ] [ baba (from Hindi) = an Indian saint or sage, babaji = baba+ji. 'ji' is a suffix used to show respect]. Babas or saints in India are virtuous people who abandon worldly pleasures but recently some fake saints have become disgraceful in the name of babas or saints.

10.
Ans.-

Wright Town
Jabalpur (MP)
17 July 2015

The Editor
The Hitvad
RusselChowkJabalpur (MP)

Respected Sir,

Subject: My concern about People's blind faith in dhongi babas

Through your esteemed column Public Opinion Forum, I want to express my concern about people's faith in dhongi babas and consequent rape victims who had to suffer due to their superstitions.
I am surprised how some educated people in this age of science and technology become prey to these predatory babas. What perplexes me most is that people surrender the whole of their family at the feet of baba ji. They become so blind in faith that they don't want to listen to anything against their guru ji. If you examine closely, you will find that a lot of highly educated people are beelining to get the blessing of these fake babajis.

I don't think God will be served better with the help of these babajis. Hinduism is the best religion in the world because it tells the easiest ways to worship God without even going to the temple of these babaji. You can do the best worship of God at home itself. There are several scriptures and several methods of worship in them. Why should we not rely on them?

I think the reason is something else. People are sentimental, lazy and greedy. They don't want to work and wait. Everybody wants shortcuts and consequently starts believing in miracles. And here comes the role of these fake babajis who claim or pretend to do miracles. Sometimes, they don't claim any miracles but people see miracles or spiritual power in them.

I am surprised what the use of all their basic science is that they have learnt in their student life. I reiterate that there is nothing miracle in this world. Don't believe in luck or fortune. All the luck is in your hand. You are the creator of your destiny. You can change yourself. Believe in yourself not in these babas.

I request all the citizens to have scientific and rational thinking which can really help us and teach your children likewise.

Thank you.

Yours faithfully,


Rajesh Ravi

11. You are Rajesh Ranjan from Wright Town Jabalpur. There are two parks in your locality, Rajendra Park and Vivekanand Park. But these parks have been taken over by antisocial elements and the result is that nobody likes to go to these parks. People are afraid of the antisocial elements always present there. Write a letter

to the Editor of a local newspaper expressing concern over the misuse of these parks.
Ans.-

Wright Town
Jabalpur (MP)
17 July 2015

The Editor
The Hitvad
Russel Chowk Jabalpur (MP)

Respected Sir,

Subject: Parks of Wight Town occupied by antisocial elements.
I am writing to express my concern about the misuse of the two parks of Wright Town Jabalpur. I am a resident of Write Town Jabalpur but presently I am working as a computer engineer in Hyderabad. I used to visit these parks when I was here but today I visited Vivekanand Park after a long interval. I was pained to see the plight of this park. I did not find the usual scene that I used to see: elderly people in groups sitting and chatting, young children hopping here and there and playing, students sitting under the trees reading books. Men and women all visited the parks. But I saw antisocial elements gambling here. Some of them were taking drugs also. There was a complete absence of gentle folks from the park. Empty bottles of wine were scattered here and there.
Almost the same plight was observed in Rajendra Park also. I found antisocial elements horse playing, hitting and abusing one another. Some of them were drunk also.
Perhaps, unabated entry of antisocial elements in the parks has forced gentlefolk to keep distance from it.

I raise my concern through your paper and draw the attention of the concerned authorities to take appropriate action so that these parks may be freed from these antisocial elements.
Thank you.

Yours faithfully,


Rajesh Ranjan


12. Write an order for books to S. Chand & Company Ram Nagar Delhi.
Ans.-

Adarsh Nagar Katni
17 July 2015

S. Chand & Company
Ramnagar New Delhi

Dear Sir,

Subject: Order for books.

I wish to buy the following books. Please send them to my address by VPP. I am sending a DD of Rs 500 in advance. The remainder amount shall be paid on receiving the books.
List of books:-
1. English Grammar and Composition by Wren and Martin.
2. Written Communication by Sarah Freeman
3. Living English Structure by W.S. Allen
Thanking you,

Yours faithfully,


Rajesh Kumar Jain

**Useful and Important Sentences for formal Letter to the Head of Any Department**

1.      I am writing to express my sincere gratitude for your support and assistance.

2.      I would like to formally request a meeting to discuss the following matters in detail.

3.      Please find attached the documents pertaining to the issue discussed.

4.      I am writing to bring to your attention a matter of utmost importance.

5.      I would appreciate it if you could provide further clarification on this matter.

6.      I am writing to follow up on my previous correspondence dated (date).

7.      Your prompt response to this matter would be highly appreciated.

8.      I am seeking your approval for the proposed plan outlined in the attached document.

9.      Kindly review the attached proposal and provide your feedback at your earliest convenience.

10.     I am writing to request an extension of the deadline for the current project.

11.     I would like to express my interest in the vacant position within your department.

12.     Please let me know a suitable time for us to discuss this matter further.

13.     I am writing to formally submit my resignation from my current position, effective (date).

14.     I would be grateful if you could address this issue as soon as possible.

15.     I am writing to request your authorization for the proposed budget.

16.     I am reaching out to seek your guidance on a matter of significant concern.

17.     Your consideration and approval of this request would be greatly appreciated.

18.     I would like to propose a meeting to discuss the recent developments in the department.

19.     I am writing to request your support for the upcoming project.

20.     Please inform me of the next steps required to proceed with this initiative.

21.     I am writing to report an incident that occurred on (date).

22.     I would appreciate it if you could expedite the processing of this request.

23.     I am writing to seek your advice on a strategic decision we are facing.

24.     I am writing to notify you of my decision to retire, effective (date).

25.     I would like to thank you for your consideration of my proposal.

26.     I am writing to express my concerns regarding the current situation.

27.     Please provide your approval for the attached schedule at your earliest convenience.

28.     I am writing to request additional resources for our ongoing project.

29.     Your timely intervention in this matter would be greatly appreciated.

30.     I am writing to request a formal evaluation of my performance.

31.     I would like to request a transfer to a different department within the organization.

32.     I am writing to express my willingness to collaborate on the upcoming project.

33.     Please let me know if there are any additional documents required.

34.     I am writing to bring to your notice a discrepancy in the recent report.

35.     I would like to discuss the implementation of the new policy at your convenience.

36.     I am writing to request approval for my upcoming leave of absence.

37.     Your prompt attention to this urgent matter is necessary.

38.     I am writing to request a reconsideration of your previous decision.

39.     Please advise on the best course of action to resolve this issue.

40.     I am writing to inform you of my decision to resign from my position, effective immediately.

41.     I am seeking your permission to attend the upcoming conference on (date).

42.     I would appreciate your feedback on the attached draft proposal.

43.     I am writing to notify you of a potential conflict of interest.

44.     Please confirm receipt of this letter at your earliest convenience.

45.     I am writing to propose a new initiative that could benefit our department.

46.     Your approval of this request will enable us to proceed without delay.

47.     I am writing to request a detailed report on the current status of the project.

48.     I would like to discuss the budget allocation for the upcoming fiscal year.

49.     I am writing to request a reconsideration of my application for the position.

50.     Please feel free to contact me if you require any further information.

**Exercise-3.**

1. Write an application to the Collector of your city about movement of loaded trucks in the city within the no entry time of the trucks.
2. Write an application to the Commissioner of Municipal Corporation of your city about the encroachment of a park in your locality.
3. Write an application to the M.L.A. of your constituency complaining about the increase in the number of slum dwellers near your residence.
4. Write a letter to the Editor of an esteemed newspaper expressing your concern about increasing air pollution of your city due to vehicular and industrial smoke.
5. Write an application to the Police Commissioner / Superintendent of your city about the increasing number of instances of theft and police being unable to curb them.
6. Write an application to the Collector of your city about the noise pollution created by DJ on the road just to attract the attention of the people.
7. Write a letter of complaint to the Commissioner of Municipal Corporation of your city about poor roads of your colony and water logging in the streets.
8. Write a letter to the Editor of an esteemed daily newspaper about mob lynching of a person who was an innocent beggar and who was suspected to be child trafficker. Express your concern about people taking law in their hand.
9. Write a letter to the Editor of an esteemed daily newspaper about the nexus between private school management and book sellers with a view to exploiting the parents.
10. Write a letter of complaint to The Police Commissioner of your city about the hoodlums creating nuisance in your colony by rash driving in groups and shouting.

# Part 6

# *Application Letter for Job Résumé / C.V. writing*

## *This Part Contains Application Letter for Job Résumés/C.V.'s Kinds of Résumés And Several Samples*

# Application Letter for job

After you have completed your graduation, the first thing that you will need to do is to write an application letter for a job.

Your application letter for a job is your first impression and first examination in the job getting process. That is why you need to write the application letter for the job carefully. The more so, because, if your application fails the very first examination, you have no further chances of being recruited. Therefore an application letter for job must be written with due care and proper planning.

This process involves writing a covering letter and a resume. In other words you have to write two letters: a letter called 'covering letter' and another letter called 'résumé'.

## Covering Letter

A covering letter is very much similar to a formal letter. It mentions the source of the information of the vacancy against which you are applying. You give a brief introduction of yourself, your qualification, your experience and your suitability for the post. You formally apply for the post here.

## Résumé

A résumé is a summary of academic performance, work history and other relevant information about a person who is applying for a position in an organization.

A résumé contains a detailed account about your personal information like your name, your father's name, your contact address, phone numbers, your hobbies, your marital status, and information about your academic qualifications, extracurricular activities, experience/ trainings taken, seminars/conferences attended/given and awards received.

A résumé is in fact a supporting document to the covering letter. A covering letter cannot have detailed information about you. It gives only a brief introduction of yourself. Therefore, detailed information is given in the résumé.

**Note-**For writing an application letter for a job you need to write two letters one covering letter and other résumé. Writing only a covering letter or résumé is not appropriate. Remember that a résumé must be preceded by a covering letter. In other words, a covering letter must be supported by a résumé.

# <u>Lay out of a résumé</u>

## Personal profile

Name-

Father's Name-

Date of Birth-                                             Age-

Nationality-

Marital status

Address for correspondence

Permanent Address

Contact No

E-mail Address

## Academic Profile

| SN | Degree/ Diploma/ Certificate | Board/ University | Year of passing | Division/ Percentage | Subjects | Distinction |
|----|----|----|----|----|----|----|
|  |  |  |  |  |  |  |
|  |  |  |  |  |  |  |
|  |  |  |  |  |  |  |
|  |  |  |  |  |  |  |

## Extracurricular Profile

| SN | Activity | Year | Rank/Place |
|----|----------|------|------------|
|    |          |      |            |
|    |          |      |            |

**Hobbies**
**Seminars attended**

**Experience Profile**

| SN | Period From.........To............. | Designation | Organisation ................... | Salary................. |
|----|------------------------------------|-------------|----------------------------------|------------------------|
|    |                                    |             |                                  |                        |
|    |                                    |             |                                  |                        |

**Awards and achievements**
**References**

Date
Signature
Place

# Writing a Résumé

Above, you have seen a simple procedure of writing a résumé. Remember that there is no hard and fast rule for writing résumé. It is simply a sales letter. You write this letter because you want to sell your services. Your objective is to catch the attention of the employer according to your suitability to a particular job. Therefore you can arrange different items of information about you in the order which attracts the employer most. You can highlight you experience first if you feel that your employer should be interested more in your experience than in other profiles. For such a résumé, you should write your experience first, and then awards, seminars, then academic profile and the personal profile would come at the end. The order of various items of information about you is your personal choice, which you have to decide keeping your audience in your mind. Thus writing a résumé is an art and there are various methods of writing it.

# Sample Application Letters for Job
## Sample 1

**Question.** You are Yashwant Sharma B.Tech. Mechanical from IIT Kharagpur and MBA from IIM Ahmedabad. You have been working for five years in Blue Diamond Cement Pvt. Ltd. Satna (MP) as production Manager (mechanical). You have also worked as Assistant Production Manager for three years in KP Cement Ltd. KayPee Nagar Sagar (MP). Write a letter of application to Brazim Cement Ltd. Chandrapur (Rajasthan) for the post of Vice-President (Production).

**Answer.-**

# An Application Letter for Job
## Covering Letter

**12 Adarsha Nagar**

**Satna (MP)**
**3 November, 2007**

**The Manager HRD**
**Brazim Cement Ltd**
**Chandrapur (Rajasthan)**

Dear Sir,

Subject-Application for the post of Vice-President (Production)

In response to your advertisement placed in The Ascent (The Times of India Dated 26 Oct, 2007), I present myself as a candidate for the post of Vice-President (Production)

I am presently working as Production Manager in Blue Diamond Cement Ltd. Satna. Previously, I have worked as an Assistant Manager Production in KP Cement Ltd Kay Pee Nagar Sagar (MP).

I have always been interested in maximizing production cost effectively. My seven year experience has taught me a lot in this regard. I am still working in this direction and I hope that I will certainly get more successes.

I think an interview session will be more convenient to discuss these things in details.

Thanks,
Encl. - (i) Résumé
(ii)Testimonials

**Yours faithfully,**

**Yeshwant Sharma**

# Résumé

## Personal Profile

**Name**-Yeshwant Sharma
**Father**- Shree- Bihari Lal Sharma
**Date of Birth**- 10 Oct, 1978                    Age-27 years
**Nationality**- Indian
**Marital Status**- Married-One Child
**Permanent Address**- 40 Vashali Enclave Dilshad Gardsens New Delhi-110012
**Address for Correspondence**-Vasundhara 12 Adarsha Nagar Satna (MP)-485001
**Contact No**-07672 -233430=Mobile Phone-2992789635
E-mail-yashwsharma@rediffmail.com


## Academic Profile

| SN | Degree/ Diploma/ Certificate | Board /university | Year of passing | Division, percentage | Subjects | Distinction |
|---|---|---|---|---|---|---|
| 1 | High School | CBSE | 1990 | First Division 79% | Hindi, English, Science, Mathematics, Social Science | Hindi Maths |
| 2 | Higher Secondary | CBSE | 1992 | First Division 76% | Hindi, English, Mathematics, Physics, Chemistry, | English Maths Physics |
| 3 | B.Tech (Mechanical) | IIT Kharagpur | 1996 | First Division 81% | All Subjects Specialization in Production Technology | KOM. DOM PT |
| 4 | MBA | IIM Ahemdabad | 1998 | First Division 81% | All Subjects Specialization in Production Technology | PT |

## Extracurricular Activities

| SN | Activity | Year | Rank/Place |
|---|---|---|---|
| 1 | Won Inter School Football Championship as The Captain | 1991 | First |
| 2 | Won Inter School Handball Championship as The Captain | 1992 | First |
| 3 | Best Debater Award | 1993 | First |
| 4 | Best Seminar Presentation Award | 1994 | Second |
| 5 | Best Project of the year | 1995 | First |
| 6 | Group Discussion Contest | 1996 | First |

**Hobbies**- Playing Badminton, watching cricket, reading magazines.

## Experience Profile

| SN | Period From………To…… | Designation | Organization | Salary ( CTC ) |
|---|---|---|---|---|
| 1 | 7July,1998 To 5 Sep,2000 | Assistant Manager (Production) | KP Cement Ltd Sagar(MP) | Rs.1200000 per annum |
| 2 | 5 Oct,2000 Till Date | Production Manager (Manager) | Blue Diamond Cement Satna (MP) | Rs-1600000 per annum |

# References

1. Mr. Y.K. Rajan
   Principal
   IIT New Delhi
2 . Mr. S.K. Varma
   Manager (Production)
   KP Cement Sagar (MP)
3. Mr.S.P. Tewari
   Vice-President
   (Production)
   Blue Diamond Cement
   Satna (MP)

Signature

Yeshwant Sharma

Place- Satna (MP)
3 November, 2007

# Sample 2

**Question:-** Write an application letter for job in response to the following advertisement: -

<u>Sharada Cement Ltd</u>.

**Sharada Nagar Maihar (Satna) 4843321**

# Wanted

## <u>Graduate Engineer Trainees</u>

Applications are invited from

fresh engineering graduates against 20 openings

of graduate engineer trainees.

Minimum Qualifications:- BE Mech/EE/EC/IT

with at least 70% marks or equivalent.

No experience required. Freshers only.

Final year students may also apply.

Rush your application to above address or email to
sharadacement@gmail.com within a week.

**Answer:-**

6 Jawahar Nagar

**Satna (MP)**
**3 November, 2013**

**The Personnel Manager**
**Sharda Cement Ltd.**
**Sharda Nagar Maihar Satna (MP)**

Dear Sir,

Subject-Application for the post of Graduate Engineer Trainee

In response to your advertisement placed in The Ascent (The Times of India Dated 26 Oct, 2007), I present myself as a candidate for the post of Graduate Engineer Trainee.

I am a final year $8^{th}$ semester student studying at Vindhya Institute of Technology and Science Satna (MP). Overall CGP of mine is A+ which is equivalent to 80%. I have passed all the papers of engineering in first attempt.

Besides these qualifications, I have always had keen interest in extracurricular activities like Debate, Group Discussion, Seminar Presentation, football and handball.

I have undergone a three-month industrial training at Prism Cement Ltd Satna (MP) from 25 June 2013 to 24 September 2013. I feel that my training is very much relevant to the opening against which I am applying.

I think an interview session will be more convenient to discuss the relevance of my training.

Thanks,

Encl. - (i) Résumé
      (ii)Testimonials

**Yours faithfully,**

# Résumé

## Personal Profile

**Name**-Mukesh Mishra
**Father**- Shree- Jeevan Lal Mishra
**Date of Birth**- 10 Oct, 1993                    Age-20 years
**Nationality**- Indian
**Marital Status**-Unmarried
**Permanent Address**- 32 Yashodhara Enclave Boda Bag Rewa (MP)-486001
**Address for Correspondence**-Varma Bhawan 6 Jawahar Nagar Satna (MP)-485001
**Contact No**-07672 -233430=Mobile Phone-2992789635
E-mail-mukeshmishra101@rediffmail.com

## Academic Profile

| SN | Degree/ Diploma/ Certificate | Board /university | Year of passing | Division, percentage | Subjects | Distinction |
|---|---|---|---|---|---|---|
| 1 | High School | CBSE | 2008 | First Division 79% | Hindi, English, Science, Mathematics, Social Science | Hindi Maths |
| 2 | Higher Secondary | CBSE | 2010 | First Division 76% | Hindi, English, Mathematics, Physics, Chemistry, | English Maths Physics |
| 3 | B.E (Mechanical) | VITS Satna (MP) RGPV Bhopal | Due for2014 final year | First Division Overall CGPA of 7 semesters = A+ | All Subjects Specialization in Production Technology | KOM. DOM PT |

# Extracurricular Activities

| SN | Activity | Year | Rank/Place |
| --- | --- | --- | --- |
| 1 | Won Inter School Football Championship as The Captain | 2007 | First |
| 2 | Won Inter School Handball Championship as The Captain | 2008 | First |
| 3 | Best Debater Award | 2008 | First |
| 4 | Best Seminar Presentation Award | 2011 | Second |
| 5 | Best Project of the year | 2013 | First |
| 6 | Group Discussion Contest | 2013 | First |

**Hobbies**- Playing football and handball, watching cricket, and reading magazines.

# Industrial Training

I have undergone Industrial Training in summer at Prism Cement Satna (MP) from 25 June 2013 to 24 September 2013.

# Projects

I have submitted a Minor Project on Use of Robots in Sewer Blockage Cleaning 30 October 2010.

# References

1. Mr.P.C.Shrivastava
Principal
VITS Satna (MP)

2 . Mr. SantoshDwivedi
HoD Mechanical
VITS Satna (MP)

3. Mrs.Meeta Sonkar
   HoD Engineering Chemistry
   VITS  Satna(MP)

Signature

Mukesh Mishra

Place- Satna (MP)
3 November, 2007

***

# Sample 3

**Question:-** You are Rajesh Sharma living in Rajendra Nagar Satna (MP) , you have recently completed your diploma in mechanical engineering from VITS college affiliated to RGPV Bhopal. You see the following advertisement on the Ascent The Times of India. Write an application letter for job

# *Ekta Steels Pvt. Ltd.*

**Satkar Bhawan Barakhamba Road New Delhi 110007**

## Wanted

### <u>Diploma Engineer Trainees</u>

**For our state-of – the - art plant (plastic pipe unit) at New Delhi
Essential Qualification- 1. Diploma in (Production / Mechanical
Engineering). 2. Strong communication Skills in English.
Freshers too can apply however experienced candidates will get
bonus marks. Apply to the above address or Email to
ektasteelshr@yahoo.co.in**

*Answer:-*

**Rajendra Nagar Satna
10 May, 2016**

**The Personnel Manager
Ekta Steels  Pvt. Ltd.
Satkar Bhawan BaraKhamba Road
New Delhi**

**Respected Sir,**

Subject- Application for the post of Diploma Engineer Trainees

I am a diploma engineer (Mechanical) with 8.9 cgpa from
RGPV Bhopal.
I present myself as a candidate for the post of Diploma
Engineer Trainee as per your advertisement that appeared on 1
May 2016.
I promise you that I will leave no stone unturned. My strength
is my skills and hard work.

Thanks,

Yours faithfully

Rajesh

Encl. - (i) Résumé
(ii)Testimonials

# Résumé

## Personal Profile

Name- Rajesh

Father's Name – Hareesh

Address for correspondence:- 9 Rajendra Nagar Satna (MP) 485001

Contact Information:- M. 9870984568 Phone 0767289765
Rajesh45@gmail.com

## Academic Profile

1. High School 2009 Government Venkat Higher Secondary School Satna (MP) MP Board Bhopal with 81%
2. Higher Secondary 2011 Government Venkat Higher Secondary School Satna (MP) MP Board Bhopal with 79%
3. Diploma Mechanical Engineering 2014 from VITS Satna affiliated to RGPV Bhopal with 8.1 cgpa

## Extracurricular Profile

1. As the captain I have won Inter School cricket trophy in 2009
2. AS the captain, I won the handball championship in 2011.

## Industrial Training

I have taken industrial training in Satna Cement Works from 1 June 2014 to 7 July 2014

## References

1. Dr. Rajendra Singh Principal VITS Satna
2. Mr. Santosh Dwivedi HoD Mechanical Engineering
3. Mr. MP Pandey Assistant Professor Electrical VITS Satna

***

# Sample 4

**Question:-**You are Rajesh Kumar Jain residing near the city Kotwali Satna (MP). You are an M.C.A. You have one year experience of working as a computer programmer. Write an application to the Manager Universal Cables Ltd. Satna for the post of computer programmer.

**Answer.-**

**Matri Chhaya**
**Near City KotwaliSatna (MP)**
**17 July 2015**

**The Manager**
**Universal Cables Ltd. Satna (MP)**

Respected Sir,

Subject: Application for the post of computer programmer.

I have gone through the job requirements advertised by your company in the Times of India dated 15 July 2015. I find myself suitable for this post.
I am an M.C.A. from RGPV Bhopal. I am presently working as a computer programmer with Rewa Telelinks Rewa. I have a total of one year experience of working as a computer programmer. I am sure that this experience will be very useful for working in your company.
I would very much appreciate your giving me a chance to be interviewed for this post.
Thank you.

**Yours faithfully,**

**Rajesh Kumar Jain**

Encls. 1. Résum
     2. Testimonials

# Résumé

**Rajesh Kumar Jain**
Matri Chhaya
near City Kotwali Satna (MP)
Phone-+9189876459
Email-rkjsatna@rediffmail.com

# Personal Details

Father- Ravi Kumar Jain

Date of birth- 6 January 1992

Age- 24 years

Marital Status- unmarried

Nationality- Indian

| SN | Certificate/ Degree | Board/ University | Year | Division/ Percentage | Subjects |
|---|---|---|---|---|---|
| 1 | High School | MP Board | 2007 | First Division 87% | Hindi English. Math's, Science, Social Science |
| 2 | Higher Secondary | MP Board | 2009 | First Division 82% | Hindi English. Math's, Physics, Chemistry |
| 3 | BCA | Makhanlal Chaturvedi National University Bhopal | 2012 | First Division 77% | Foundation Hindi English. General Awareness All subjects (computer application) |
| 4 | MCA | IGNOU | 2014 | First Division 75% | All subjects (computer application) |

# Education

| SN | From…..to | Designation | Institution |
|---|---|---|---|
| 1 | 2 August 2014 to 31 June 2015 | Computer Programmer | Vindhya Telelinks Ltd Rewa |

# Experience

## References

(1)     R.P. Goswami
Ex-Principal
Saraswati HS
School Satna (MP)

(2)     Dr.B.S. Parihar
Director (Coordinator)
IGNOU Study Center Satna

(3)      S.P. Agrawal
         Personnel Manager
         Vindhya Telelinks Ltd Rewa

         Signature

         Rajesh Kumar Jain

         Place- Satna
         Date- 17 July 2015


****

# Résumé, C.V. or Bio-data

These three words are generally taken as substitutes for each other however the conventions have created differences in them. Nowadays, bio-data is used for marriage purposes. It is only résumé or CV that is now used for employment purposes.

****

# Résumé or C.V. (Curriculum Vitae)

Meaning of résumé or C.V. is the same however there is some difference also. We use résumé for professional purposes when we apply for a job against an opening. While on the other hand, we use C.V. for academic purposes. If you are applying against an academic opening and you have to mention your research record or you want to become a research scholar, you should use C.V or Curriculum Vitae. Similarly, if you are applying against an opening which is non-academic or professional or technical, you can use the word résumé. Besides this difference, a résumé is concise by its nature whereas a C.V. has much detailed description of educational and professional achievements.

# Categorization of information in a résumé

### Different Sections of a Résumé

A résumé is important because it categorizes the information under certain sections and makes it easier for the employer to go into a certain section and view relevant or most important information as per his choice.

Generally, a résumé distributes the information into the following sections / points:-

### Personal Profile /Personal Information /Contact information

You can write here your name, father's name, date of birth, age, matrimonial status, address for correspondence, permanent address, phone number, email etc. It is not necessary that you must give two addresses. You may give only one i.e. address for correspondence. It is also possible that your permanent address and address for correspondence may be the same. The purpose of matrimonial status is that it requires mentioning whether you are married or unmarried and the status of your family because the employer gives certain family benefits.

**Objective(s) / Short Profile (Summary of your experience): -** Writing objective is, in fact, not necessary. If you mention several objectives, it may give the notion that you are confused about your objectives and it raises the question where your focal point lies. It is not right to write the same objective(s) for different positions. If you are writing objective/s, it/they must be in conformity with the job requirement and you will need to change it for a different job. Make it simple and realistic. Don't write unrealistic fancy objectives. They will actually harm you. You shall be asked questions about them in the interview. It is better to write a short profile about your experience and nature of your work rather than objective(s). Remember that hiring managers give hardly a minute in examining your résumé. Nobody is concerned what your objective(s) is/are but the employer would certainly like to know the profile of your work. Thus a short profile will work better.

**Skills and Competencies: -** You have to mention skills and competencies that you have acquired through your education or your experience.

**Educational qualifications: -** You can mention your educational qualifications in chronological order starting from High School to the highest qualification or in a reverse chronological order starting from the highest qualification to your High School qualification. Besides this you must mention the 'Board or University', 'Year of Passing', 'the percentage of your marks' or 'grade' or 'CGPA' and the subjects you offered. It is better to present these qualifications in a table form.

**Activities, interests and hobbies: -** You may mention your interests/activities/ interests also however you must know that these hobbies must not be hindrances to the job of the company where you wish to work otherwise it is better not to mention them. Besides this, if you don't possess any hobby or interest or you have only workable knowledge of any pursuit, it is better not to mention it because you may have to face questions relating to it in the interview.

**Projects Undertaken: -** If you have undertaken any projects, in your academic session, or as a part of your regular work, you should mention it giving its details about the name of the project, nature, duration and its outcome.

**Industrial Training: -** If you have undergone any industrial training or apprenticeship you must mention it; especially if you are a fresher because it will work like experience and if it is relevant to the job you have applied for, you have greater chances of getting the job.

**Work Experience: -** You have to inform the employer about your experience. You have to mention the name of the company where you are working, your designation, duration of your work, since when you have been working and your salary/CTC. (CTC=Cost to company = Your annual salary and all the benefits that you get from the company in a year).

If you have worked at more than one place, you can present this information in a table format in the columns of 'name of organization', 'designation', 'duration-(from ......to)' and 'salary/CTC'.

**Rewards and Achievements: -** If you have been awarded for your achievements, you must mention them with details of achievements. It will be an extra feather in your cap.

**References: -** You have to provide the names and addresses of three persons with whom you have worked for the purpose of reference so that the employer may confirm information provided by you and the quality of your performance.

These sections are generally written in the order mentioned above. This is a popular sequence. However, this is not a rigid sequence. One can change this sequence depending on the fact which section he wants to highlight most. Most important section which he wants to highlight should come first and other less important ones may follow it.

# Kinds of Résumés

Depending upon qualification, work experience, objective and personal circumstances, several types of résumés are written. Some of them are traditional and others are nontraditional.

# Traditional Résumés

Traditionally the following five kinds of résumés have been popular in the world of work:-

**Chronological Résumé**
**Functional Résumé**
**Combination Résumé**
**Résumé with profile section**
**Targeted Résumé**

***

# Chronological Résumé

A chronological Résumé lists your work history and academic qualifications in reverse chronological order. It starts from the present and goes back into the past in reverse order. If you have solid work history and quantification without gap, this type of résumé will serve best for you. Employers too prefer this type of résumé because it is convenient for the employer to track all your work history and qualifications systematically.

### A sample Chronological Résumé

# Vishal Bharadwaj

**6 Adarsh Nagar Satna (MP) 486001**
**07672-224115 (home)**
**89695489&5 (cell)**
**email-vhshalbharadwaj22@gmail.com**

## Experience
**April 2009 - Present**
**Manager Production,**
Blue Diamond Cement Satna (MP)
Increased the production of cement from 100 ton per to 175 ton per day
Made it cost effective by 16%
Reported to Mr. R.S. Rawat General Manager Production
**July 2007 - April 2009**
**Assistant Manager Production,**
Swastika Cement Katni (MP)
Got a break as Assistant Manager after doing my degree in production technology through a campus interview.
Reported to Mr. Gagan Pratap Singh Manager Production
Learnt cost effective production from him
## Education
**July 2007**
Bachelor of Technology in Production Technology, Radisson Institute of Technology Bairagarh Bhopal (MP)
**July 2003**

Senior Secondary School Certificate Examination from DPS
Agra
**July 2001**
High School Certificate Examination from DPS Agra
**Computer Skills**
Experience with social media and internet search, MS Word,
PPT and Excel
**References**:-
Shree Ram Shankar Rawat
General Manager Production
Blue Diamond Cement Satna (MP)

Mr. Gagan Pratap Singh
Manager Production
Sawastika Cement Katni (MP)

Mr. Ravindra Rai
The Principal
Radisson Institute of Technology
Bairagarh Bhopal

Signature


Vishal Bharadwaj
Place- Kanpur
Date- 17 July 2010


***


# Functional Résumé

A Functional Résumé emphasizes on your skills and experience rather than your chronological history of work. If you have gaps in your work history, and /or education, you should prefer this type of résumé.

**<u>A Sample Functional Résumé</u>**

# NiteshVerma

**15 Right Town Jabalpur 483001**
**Phone: 9893459823**
**Email: niteshverma23@yáhoo.co.in**

**OBJECTIVE –** To obtain a position where I can maximize my multilayer of technical skills i.e. Quality Assurance Program Development. training and experience of customer service and a successful track record in the maintenance of a cement plant.

## SUMMARY OF QUALIFICATIONS

Result oriented, high energy, hands on experience of plant maintenance (crushing, milling and packing) with a successful record of preventive maintenance of plants, quality assurance, computer program development, customer service and training of the new employees in the plant.

Major strengths include strong leadership, excellent communication skills, competent strong team player, attention to details, dutiful respect for compliance in all regulated environments and supervisory skills including hiring, termination, scheduling, training, payroll and other administrative tasks. Thorough knowledge of current production practices and a clear vision to accomplish the company goals. Computer and internet literate.

## PROFESSIONAL ACCOMPLISHMENTS

<u>Plant Manager Crushing Plant</u>

Looking after the operation and maintenance of LimeStone Crusher ACC Cement Katni for five years. No breakdown reported till now.

Maintaining the plant as per Six Sigma Quality Certification and reporting to Vice President Production and got award for cost effective techniques applied in the plant.

## Manager Milling Plant

Supervised milling plant for its operation and maintenance and reported to the In-charge of milling plant at ACC Cement Katni for three years. Successful operation and no breakdown during my tenure.

Maintained the record of maintenance as per Six Sigma Quality Certification.

## Head Trainer

Trained new recruits at the Head Office in Mumbai and the Best Teacher Award was conferred on me.

## EDUCATION

M. Tech Mechanical Engineering from IIT New Delhi

B.E. Mechanical Engineering from University Institute of Technology Bhopal(MP)

SSC from Emerald Heights International School Indore (MP)

High School from Emerald Heights International School Indore (MP)

## REFERENCES

Shree Deepak Sahni
Vice President Production
ACC Cement Katni (MP)

Mr. Rakesh Pratap Singh
General Manager Production
ACC Cement Katni (MP)

Mr. George Elvis
The Principal
Indian Institute of Technology
New Delhi

Signature

Nitesh Verma
Place- Jabalpur
Date- 7 July 2010

***

# Combination Résumé

Combination Résumé as the name indicates is, in fact, a combination of chronological and functional résumés. It lists your skills and experience first and your employment history next. With this type of résumé, you can highlight your skills and experience which are relevant and provide the chronological work history that employers prefer.

<u>**Sample Combination Résumé**</u>

# Raj KishorVatsakar

**33 Rachana Apartments  Kidwai Nagar Kanpur (UP)**
**Phone +91790665474 Email rkvatsakar@gmail.com**

I am interested in pursuing a career in software development. I consider myself a fast learner and a team player. I feel that I can make a contribution to any Implementation Services Department.

## Computer Skills

**Machines:**
IBM PC Compatibles, Rockwell ACD, Macintosh

**Languages:**
VBA, BASIC, Turbo, Pascal, DB/c, Turbo C, COBOL

**Programs:**
MS Access, MS Word, MS Excel, MS Outlook, Crystal Reports, MS Internet Explorer, Netscape Navigator, Support Magic, Norton Utilities

**Operating Systems:** MS Vista, MS XP, MS Windows, SCO UNIX, MS DOS Hardware: Experienced with installation of motherboards, SIMM chips, internal/external modems, NICs, SCSI and IDE hard disks, SCSI floppy drives, SCSI I/O ports, and various printer configurations.

## Experience

**1998 to Present**
**Kamal Resorts International, Kanpur (UP)**
**System Developer**

Responsible for migration of extensive file Pro database to MS Access utilizing tables, queries, forms, reports, macros, modules, and VBA. Troubleshoot and maintain existing MS Access database for Telemarketing Dept. Troubleshoot and diagnose UNIX, filePro, PC, and MS Windows related problems for in-house staff.

**1995 to 1998**
**Ultra-complex Systems, Kanpur (UP)**
**Support Engineer**

Troubleshoot and debug minor program bugs. Modify existing programs with enhancements. Implement fixes and enhancements. Design, create, and implement ticket designs. Perform remote upgrades of Proto Base and Select-a-Seat. Resolve problems and questions from Technical Support. Provide documentation. Assist Select-a-Seat Team Leader with creation and testing of new software.

## Previous Positions

**Senior Technical Support Representative**
**Technical Support Representative**
**Technical Support Operator**
**1988 to 1995**
**People's Shopping Network, Lucknow**
**Help Desk Supervisor**

Manage the Help Desk function as well as prioritizing, resolving, recognizing, and routing end-user computer problems. Establish and document policy and procedure.

**Previous positions:**
**Help Desk Operator II**
**Assistant Data Systems Analyst**
**Telecommunications Systems Operator**
**Customer Service Phone Monitor Trainer**

Network representative

# Education

1990 to 1994- B.Tech Computer Science and Engineering UPTU Lucknow
1988 to 1990- Intermediate from DAV Senior Secondary School Lucknow
1986 to 1988- High School from DAV Senior Secondary School Lucknow

# Extracurricular Activities

Winner of Sampurnanand Debate Competition- 1998
Winner of Best Project of the year Award-1993

# References

Shree Rajesh Arya
Manager Kamal Resorts International
Kanpur

Mr. Ravi Nigam
Manager Ultra-complex Systems
Kanpur

Mr. Mahesh Satpathi
The Principal
Aditya Institute of Technology
Lucknow

Signature

Raj KishorVatskar
Place- Kanpur
Date- 3 July 2000

***

# Résumé with a Profile

A résumé with a profile section includes a summary of an applicant's skills, experience and goals as they relate to a specific job. It creates a very good first impression and the employer can notice the ideal candidate from its short profile in the beginning of the résumé. The short profile can be titled by any suitable name as 'overview' ,'summary of experience' etc.

## Résumé with a Profile

# Rajneesh Kumar Jaiswal

**Matrachhaya 33 Wright Town Jabalpur (M.P) 682001**
rkjiaiswal@gmail.com
**Phone Home 0773-455553 Cell 8605550887**

## Overview

An excellent teacher of English Language and Literature. Specially interested in teaching English Grammar and Pronunciation. An amicable guide and counselor with extensive experience of teaching and advising high school/middle school students. Fluent in Hindi and English; skilled at communicating and developing relationships with ESL students and their families. Excellent written and oral communication skills.

## Education

Master of English, University of Jabalpur- 2007 - 2009
Bachelor of Arts, University of Jabalpur- 2003 - 2005
Bachelor of Education, Awadhesh Pratap Singh Vishwavidyalaya Rewa- 2005-2007

## Related Experience

**Lecturer English and Guidance Counsellor,**
**St. Mary Senior Secondary School Indore**
**Sept. 2009 – Present**

• Teach English Language, Grammar and Literature to the students of VIII, IX, X, XI, and XII.

• Meet individually with students to discuss courses, grades, behaviour, college applications, and other issues and concerns

• Maintain contact with parents and guardians of students to develop a network of support and communication around each student

• Implemented use of new data program in the counselling office to help counsellors track student progress

**Assistant teacher and Counsellor,**
**Levine Academy, Indore**
**Sept. 2007 – July 2009**
• Taught English Language, Grammar and Literature to the students of VI, VII, VIII, IX, and X.
•Counselled the middle and high school students regarding their progress and support from the teachers and parents.
• Organized college admission visits to the high school; moderated Q&A sessions and organized student interviews

**References: -**
Mr. Roger Gardener
The Principal
St. Mary Senior Secondary School Indore

Mr. Rajneesh Jaiswal
Principal
Levin Academy Indore

Mr. Ratnesh Ahuja
The Principal
University of Jabalpur

Signature


Rajneesh Kumar Jaiswal
Place- Indore
Date- 17 July 2011

***

# Targeted Resume

A targeted résumé is a résumé that is customized so that it specifically highlights the experience and skills you have that are relevant to the job you are applying for. It definitely takes more work to write a targeted resume than to just click to apply with your existing resume. However, it's well worth the effort, especially when applying for jobs that are a perfect match for your qualifications and experience.

## Sample Targeted Resume

# Ravi Shankar Bajpayee

## 32 Civil Lines Jabalpur (MP) 483002

home: 07545525 cell: 5664862222

email: email@xmail.com

## SUMMARY OF PROFESSIONAL QUALIFICATIONS

Experienced manager with expertise in human relations and human resource management. Extensive background in staff recruitment and retention. Staff training and development. Superb written and oral communication skills. Organizational and Strategic Planning. Management Coaching, Program Marketing. Contract negotiation and compliance. Knowledge of Company and Labour Law

**PROFESSIONAL AFFILIATIONS** All India Professional and Management Association Institution of Engineers

## PROFESSIONAL EXPERIENCE

### JOINT GENERAL MANAGER HRD

### Swastika Cement Ltd. Katni (MP) 2005 to Present

Responsible for recruiting, orienting, training and supervising 50 staff, was able to reduce staff turnover from 68% to 14% by improving staff orientation and training, professional development, and mid-level management coaching. Oversight of all aspects of staff performance, performance evaluation, progressive discipline, mediation of staff disputes and grievance. Leadership in the setting and achieving of strategic and organizational goals. Established training programs for staff in regard to all aspects of workplace performance and professional development program, marketing, increased annual revenue by38%.

## MANAGER HRD

### Blue Diamond Cement Sagar (MP), 2000-2005

Administrative and human resources management of a cement plant; 60 full time employees and 45 contract employees housed in various locations. Responsible for the recruitment and supervision and performance evaluation of administrative and engineering staff. Provided training to enhance workplace performance at all levels of staffing. Nominated as Training Coordinator for the whole group cement plants, providing training as the trainer or contracting with relevant professionals to provide training in the areas of engineering services, professional ethics and law, and areas of professional development as requested by staff members. Concurrently completed a two-year certificate program in Organizational Development and Leadership as the recipient of a merit scholarship by the Microsoft Corporation. Independent Consultant to several small businesses, law firms, non-profit agencies and school districts on staff grievance procedures, team building and the setting and achieving of organizational goals.

## ASSISTANT MANAGER HRD
### Laxmi Cement Katch Gujrat, 1998-2000

Responsible for the recruitment and supervision and performance evaluation of administrative and engineering staff and reported to The Manager HRD


## EDUCATION

MBA from Prestige Institute of Management Indore (MP) 1996 to 1998

B.E from Laxmi Narayan College of Technology Bhopal (MP) 1992 to 1996

SSC from Emerald Heights International School Indore (MP) 1990 to 1992

High School from Emerald Heights International School Indore (MP) 1988 to 1990

## REFERENCES:-

Shree Naresh Dixit
Vice President
Swastika Cement Ltd. Katni (MP)

Mr. Rudra Pratap Singh

General Manager HRD
Blue Diamond Cement Sagar (MP)

Mrs. Sarita Chauhan
Manager HRD
Laxmi Cement KatchGujrat

Signature


Ravi Shankar Vajpayee
Place- Katni
Date- 15 July 2006


***


# Non-traditional Résumés


Non-traditionally résumés are the résumés which you upload to a website. There are several websites like naukri.com, monster.com, timesjob.com etc where you can upload your résumé. Generally, these websites require that you fill up a form which takes all the necessary and relevant information from you. You can upload a word file of your résumé also. You can search for a job or you get notification of a job and then you can apply for the job. You can also write a cover letter while applying for a job. The employer can see all the information which you have uploaded through the form and besides this, he can get the word file of your résumé as well. If you are unemployed and are looking for a job, you must make use of this facility which is free of charge. Job Sites don't take any charge for uploading your résumé there and send notifications of the jobs relevant to you.

# Vidéo Résumés

The internet has brought about many changes in the presentation of the résumés. The résumés are getting smarter day by day. People are now uploading video résumés to the job sites. A video the résumé is the résumé presented by the candidate himself in the form of a presentation by himself. Besides this, he can upload videos displaying his achievements, award ceremonies and other important events. A video résumé is much better because it makes a better impression and the employer can watch the personality of the person. He can see how the person speaks and presents the facts before the audience. If you have strong spoken skills, you must go in for a video the résumé.

# Designer Résumés

If you search the internet for résumé templates, you will find several websites offering predesigned templates of résumés. You can download a template and transfer information at pre-decided places on the template and build your own résumé in minutes. You can log in to Canva and in this website also you can build your résumé on pre-designed templates simply by changing their information and downloading your résumé.

Besides the above, if you have MS Word skills, you can build a designer résumé like the above ones on MS Word also. MS Word also provides several templates with the help of which you can build your résumé. Before you build your résumé on MS Word, you must know that these résumés are different in the style of presentation only from the ones I have shown you. Most importantly, what you need to know is that there is no hard and fast rule to categorize and place the information on the résumé. You are free to decide according to your choice. The idea is that you must get noticed. How you do it is not important. On the internet, you can see several samples and then decide your own design.

*** 

**Useful and Important Sentences for Application Letter for Job**

1.      I am writing to express my sincere gratitude for your support and assistance.
2.      I would like to formally request a meeting to discuss the following matters in detail.
3.      Please find attached the documents pertaining to the issue discussed.
4.      I am writing to bring to your attention a matter of utmost importance.
5.      I would appreciate it if you could provide further clarification on this matter.
6.      I am writing to follow up on my previous correspondence dated (date).
7.      Your prompt response to this matter would be highly appreciated.
8.      I am seeking your approval for the proposed plan outlined in the attached document.
9.      Kindly review the attached proposal and provide your feedback at your earliest convenience.
10.     I am writing to request an extension of the deadline for the current project.
11.     I would like to express my interest in the vacant position within your department.

12.     Please let me know a suitable time for us to discuss this matter further.
13.     I am writing to formally submit my resignation from my current position, effective (date).
14.     I would be grateful if you could address this issue as soon as possible.
15.     I am writing to request your authorization for the proposed budget.
16.     I am reaching out to seek your guidance on a matter of significant concern.
17.     Your consideration and approval of this request would be greatly appreciated.
18.     I would like to propose a meeting to discuss the recent developments in the department.
19.     I am writing to request your support for the upcoming project.
20.     Please inform me of the next steps required to proceed with this initiative.
21.     I am writing to report an incident that occurred on (date).
22.     I would appreciate it if you could expedite the processing of this request.
23.     I am writing to seek your advice on a strategic decision we are facing.
24.     I am writing to notify you of my decision to retire, effective (date).
25.     I would like to thank you for your consideration of my proposal.
26.     I am writing to express my concerns regarding the current situation.
27.     Please provide your approval for the attached schedule at your earliest convenience.
28.     I am writing to request additional resources for our ongoing project.
29.     Your timely intervention in this matter would be greatly appreciated.

30.	I am writing to request a formal evaluation of my performance.
31.	I would like to request a transfer to a different department within the organization.
32.	I am writing to express my willingness to collaborate on the upcoming project.
33.	Please let me know if there are any additional documents required.
34.	I am writing to bring to your notice a discrepancy in the recent report.
35.	I would like to discuss the implementation of the new policy at your convenience.
36.	I am writing to request approval for my upcoming leave of absence.
37.	Your prompt attention to this urgent matter is necessary.
38.	I am writing to request a reconsideration of your previous decision.
39.	Please advise on the best course of action to resolve this issue.
40.	I am writing to inform you of my decision to resign from my position, effective immediately.
41.	I am seeking your permission to attend the upcoming conference on (date).
42.	I would appreciate your feedback on the attached draft proposal.
43.	I am writing to notify you of a potential conflict of interest.
44.	Please confirm receipt of this letter at your earliest convenience.
45.	I am writing to propose a new initiative that could benefit our department.
46.	Your approval of this request will enable us to proceed without delay.
47.	I am writing to request a detailed report on the current status of the project.

48.     I would like to discuss the budget allocation for the upcoming fiscal year.

49.     I am writing to request a reconsideration of my application for the position.

50.     Please feel free to contact me if you require any further information.

Important sentences for an application letter for job and resume.

1.     I am writing to express my interest in the (Job Title) position advertised on (Website/Source).

2.     Please find attached my resume for your review.

3.     I am excited about the opportunity to join (Company Name) as a (Job Title).

4.     I believe my skills and experience make me an ideal candidate for this position.

5.     I have a proven track record of success in (Industry/Field).

6.     I am particularly drawn to (Company Name) because of its commitment to (specific value or mission).

7.     My experience in (specific skill or field) aligns well with the requirements of this position.

8.     I have over (number) years of experience in (relevant field or industry).

9.     I possess strong skills in (specific skills relevant to the job).

10.     I am eager to contribute to (Company Name)'s success with my expertise in (specific area).

11.     My previous role at (Previous Company) has equipped me with the necessary skills for this job.

12.     I am confident in my ability to make a significant impact at (Company Name).

13.     I am highly motivated and look forward to the opportunity to contribute to your team.

14.     I have successfully managed projects in (specific area or industry).

15.     I am particularly skilled in (specific skill), which I believe will benefit your team.

16.     I am available for an interview at your earliest convenience.

17.     I have a strong background in (specific field), with a focus on (specific aspect).

18.     I am enthusiastic about the opportunity to grow and develop within (Company Name).

19.     My professional background includes significant experience in (specific task or responsibility).

20.     I am well-versed in (specific software or technology relevant to the job).

21.     My ability to (specific ability) has been demonstrated through my work at (Previous Company).

22.     I am excited about the possibility of working with such a dynamic and innovative company.

23.     My experience in (specific industry) has prepared me well for this role.

24.     I am confident that my unique blend of skills and experience will be valuable to your team.

25.     I have a strong passion for (specific industry or field), which is reflected in my career choices.

26.     I am eager to bring my expertise in (specific skill or field) to (Company Name).

27.     I have enclosed my resume for your consideration.

28.     My career achievements include (specific achievement), which I believe demonstrates my suitability for this role.

29.     I am particularly adept at (specific skill), a critical requirement for this position.

30.     I look forward to discussing how my skills and experiences align with your needs.

31.     I am confident that I can contribute positively to (Company Name)'s goals.

32.     I have a solid understanding of (specific field), which I am excited to apply at (Company Name).
33.     My education in (specific field or degree) has provided me with a strong foundation for this role.
34.     I am committed to continuous learning and professional development.
35.     I am enthusiastic about the challenges this role presents.
36.     I have a track record of effectively collaborating with cross-functional teams.
37.     I am skilled in (specific skill), which I am eager to apply in this position.
38.     I am writing to apply for the (Job Title) position as advertised on (Job Board/Website).
39.     I am dedicated to delivering high-quality results and exceeding expectations.
40.     I am confident that my proactive approach will be an asset to your team.
41.     I am adept at managing multiple priorities and meeting tight deadlines.
42.     I am keen to bring my skills in (specific area) to (Company Name).
43.     My professional philosophy aligns with (Company Name)'s mission and values.
44.     I am known for my ability to (specific achievement or skill), which I am eager to bring to your team.
45.     I am enthusiastic about the opportunity to leverage my skills in (specific field) at (Company Name).
46.     My enclosed resume provides further details about my background and achievements.
47.     I am eager to discuss how my background, skills, and certifications align with the needs of your team.
48.     I have consistently demonstrated my ability to (specific skill) throughout my career.

49.    I am excited about the prospect of contributing to (Company Name)'s innovative projects.

50.    I look forward to the possibility of discussing this exciting opportunity with you.

### Exercise-4.

1. Assume yourself to be Rajesh Varma MTech. in production technology from a prestigious institute and you have five-year experience of working as The Plant Manager of a steel plant. Write an application for the post of General Manager Production in Laxmi Steels Ltd Bhubaneswar. Assume remaining details by yourself.

2. You are Ashish Singh from Jabalpur. You see an advertisement of Nova Council of Science and Technology Gujrat. They require Project Manager for their science, technology and education platform. Minimum qualification is first class M.Tech and MBA besides possessing 10 year industry experience. You possess all the relevant qualifications. Write an application letter for the above post. Invent necessary details by yourself.

3. You are Ramesh Ranjan from New Delhi. You are a BE in chemical engineering and MBA in marketing. You have 20 year experience of marketing for petrochemical companies. Pragati Fertilizers requires General Manager Industrial Product Marketing. Write an application for the above post.

4. Farmers Fertilizer Cooperative Ltd Gujarat requires a Financial Management Trainee. Minimum qualifications are B.Com. 60% and C.A. You possess these qualifications. Write an application letter for the above post. Invent necessary details by yourself.

5. You are Ravi Varma MTech in mechanical engineering with 71% of marks. Aurobindo College of Engineering Kolkata requires Assistant Professor in mechanical engineering. Write an application letter for job for the above post. Invent necessary details by yourself.

6.  You Mahesh Shrivastava a first class diploma holder in electrical engineering. Ajanta Cables Jabalpur requires diploma engineer trainees. Write an application letter for the above post.

7.  As a commerce graduate, write an application letter for job for the post of accountant in a famous firm/company. Invent all the necessary details by yourself.

8.  As an engineering graduate of mechanical engineering, write an application letter for a job to Blue Diamond Cement Satna (MP) which requires Graduate Engineer Trainees in the production department. Invent all the necessary details by yourself.

9.  Blue Diamond Cement Satna (MP) requires Plant Manager for a cement mill. You are Ravindra Sethi a B.Tech in mechanical engineering from a reputed institute. You have five years experience of looking after cement mills as a plant manager. Write an application for the above post. Invent all the necessary details by yourself.

10. You are Ranjeet Singh MCA from a reputed institute. Write an application letter for a job for the post of Computer Programmer in Ajanta Cable Ltd. Rewa. Invent necessary details by yourself.

# Part 7

# *Business Correspondence*
# *or*
# *Business Letter Writing*

*This Part Contains*
*Letter inviting quotation,*
*Letter sending quotation,*
*Placing the order,*
*Letter of claim/complaint,*
*Letter of adjustment,*
*Letter of enquiry,*
*Sales letter,*
*Credit and collection letter*

# Business Correspondence

For an organization, business correspondence is as vital as air to a human being. That is why companies have separate departments or separate employees to handle the correspondence.

Many letters are written, sent and received by organizations. These letters can be divided into the following types.

(i) Letter of enquiry
(ii) Reply to a query
(iii) Inviting quotation
(iv) Sending quotation
(v) Placing the order
(vi) Letter of complaint/claim
(vii) Adjustment letter
(viii) Letter of Credit (request for credit purchase)
(ix) Collection letter
(x) Sales letter

## How to write a business letter

For correspondence, all the organizations generally provide a printed letterpad which contains a bunch of blank letters with printed letterhead. On such a letter, the name, address, phone numbers, fax number, e-mail address and website are printed on the top. The remaining part is left blank on which the text of the message is written. A business letter may have a maximum of the following items as the figure shows: -

# Structure and Layout of a business letter

1.Letter Head / Heading (Name and address of the organization)

3. Reference (Your reference & Our reference)    2. Date
4. Personal Notation
5. Inside Address
6. Attention Line
7. Salutation
8. Subject Line

9. Main body of the letter

10. Complimentary Close

12. Identification marks
13. Enclosure
14. Mailing Notation
15. C.C. (Copy to)
16. Postscript

11. Signature
(Typed name and designation)

# Elements of structure

## 1. Letterhead

This is the top side of the letter. It is an already printed part of the letter. It contains the name and address of the organization along with phone numbers, fax numbers, e-mail address, website, registration number, quality certification number, company logo, slogans etc. To give a balanced appearance to the letter, a maximum of one fifth of the total space available on the paper should be used for the letterhead. The remaining part of the letter is left blank on which the message is written.
 (See place no 1 in the figure)

The companies, which care for their reputation and good will, use good quality paper and attractive printing for the letter head. The standard of the company is reflected by its letter and the envelope.

Sometimes, the letterhead provides the place for writing the reference and the date.

But nowadays, the typist can type this information at the place according to his choice.

## 2. Date

 You have to write the date at place no 2 as shown in the figure (two spaces below the last line of the letterhead). Always spell the name of the month and the year in full figures e.g.

23 July, 2008

OR

July 23, 2008

A comma must be used to separate the date and month from the year.

Sometimes, the place of writing the date is indicated by printing the word 'date' under the letter. But nowadays, the typist has to decide where to type the date according to the style of the letter in which he wants to present it.

## 3. Reference

Every outgoing letter is assigned with a unique number and put in records for future. The Receipt and Dispatch Department of an organization keeps the record of all the incoming and outgoing letters. Every entry is maintained on the basis of this number.

This number is helpful in tracing the whole record of a letter. There is no particular system for devising this number. Every organization has its own system of assigning this number to every outgoing letter. What is important is that it should be devised in such a manner that there should be no chances of its duplicity.

You have to write this number at the place no.3 (two spaces below the date / last line of the letterhead). Sometimes the letter head may contain a place meant for writing a reference number and date. But usually, the typists type this number at the place mentioned in the figure.

Sometimes the letter may have two reference numbers i.e. 'your reference' and 'our reference'. You have to write two reference numbers when you are writing the reply of a letter. By 'Your reference' you mean to say "This is the reference number of your letter to which we are replying." Similarly, by 'Our reference' you mean to say, "This is the reference number of our letter." In case of a letter that is being written for the first time to an organization, you have to write only one reference number i.e. 'Reference'. Besides this, in case of writing a reply to a letter, instead of writing two reference numbers, you can write reference number your letter at the place of reference and then mention the reference number of the letter to which you are replying in the beginning of the main body of the letter as given below:

"Please refer to your letter number 'ORG29879' dated 24 June 2017"

To understand the importance of the reference number, you must have a general idea of business correspondence handling procedure. Every business organization has a separate Receipt and Dispatch Department which handles all the incoming and outgoing mail.

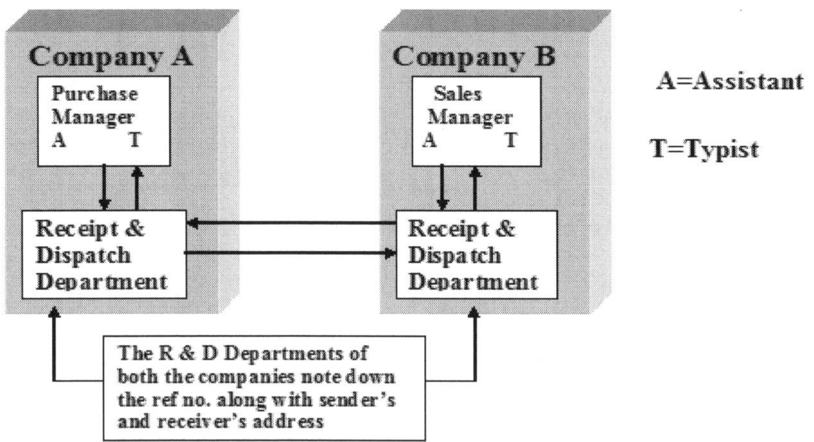


Every incoming mail does not reach a department directly but it reaches the Receipt and Dispatch Department first of all. Here, a record of the incoming mail is maintained with the help of a reference number and then it is sent to the respective head of the department who has to receive the letter. Similarly, an outgoing mail is not sent directly to the receiving organization but it is sent to the Receipt and Dispatch Department first of all. Here, a record of the outgoing mail is maintained with the help of its reference number and then it is sent to the organization which has to receive it. You must note that all the organizations may not have a separate Receipt and Dispatch Department. It depends upon the size of the organization. If the organization is small, it may have a clerk or a few people to work in the Receipt and Dispatch Department to manage incoming and outgoing mail.

This number is generated from the source by the typist. Generally every head of a department is provided with an assistant and a typist. The assistant takes the dictation of the letter from the head then he gives the content to the typist who types the letter along with assigning a reference number to the letter.

The Receipt and Dispatch Department keeps the record of all the incoming and outgoing mail. One can trace any letter with the help of its reference number.

**4. Personal Notation** (Place no 4 in the figure)If the letter is confidential, and it has to be read only by a particular person, the word <u>Personal </u>or <u>Confidential </u>is used. Such notation should appear four spaces above the inside address as well as on the envelope.

**5. Inside Address (**Place no 5 in the figure)
The inside address is the name / designation of the person and / or the address of the organization to whom the letter is being written. Generally, it starts with the designation (name in some cases). It is typed two spaces below the date / reference. It must be written without any change as such you have received from the original source (their letterhead). Any change in the address / name may be treated as an insult to the organization. Therefore, don't even abbreviate the address. Capitalize every letter of the designation and the name of the organization. In case, you have to write the name of the person, begin with Shri / Shree / Shrimati / Shreemati / Smt / Kumari / Kum /Mr /Mrs /Ms etc. Incase you have a doubt about a woman's marital status whether she is married or unmarried, use Ms. to address her. If the person has a title, use the title in place Shri /Mr.  etc or before it,  e.g. Dr. Mr. R.P.Saxena or Dr R.P.Saxena or Professor G.P.Singh. etc.

While addressing a firm Messrs is used e.g.
Messrs Daulatmal and Sons
66 Rajendra Prasad Marg
Bhopal- 440033
For the companies, Messrs is not suitable and the inside address should start with the designation of the concerned officer e.g.

The Chief Accounts Officer
Indian Aluminum Company Ltd
Lajpat Nagar
New Delhi-110011

The Personnel Manager
Diamond  Cement Ltd
BagahaSatna (MP)

Or
Shri R K Shukla
The Sales Manager
Ultratech Cement Ltd.
Sarojini Nagar Jaipur-550045
Or
The Sales Manager
Ultratech Cement Ltd.
Sarojini Nagar Jaipur-550045

## 6. Attention Line

To ensure prompt attention especially in very big organizations a line of attention is added after the inside address. It is typed two spaces below the inside address in the following manner:-
Attention: The Purchase Manager
Or
Attention: for Mr. Sudesh Gautam
Or
For the kind attention of Mr. Sudesh Gautam
It ensures the prompt delivery of the letter and immediate action on it and must be written if the organization is very big.
(See place no 6 in the figure)

## 7. Salutation

Salutation is like greeting a person when you meet him therefore it is the most formal and essential element. It helps win the reader and prepares ground for giving him any piece of information. The choice of salutation depends upon your relation with the reader.

It is typed two spaces below the inside address / attention line (See place No 7 in the figure).

Most common salutation for business correspondence is 'Dear Sir' or 'Dear Madam' if it is addressed to an individual by designation/name. In case of addressing an organization, use 'Dear Sirs' or 'Dear Madams' (if the organization consists of women only). In the USA, they use 'Gentlemen' in place of 'Dear Sirs' (but 'Gentleman' is never used).

You can opt for salutations like Dear Shree Mishraji, Dear Mrs. Sharma, Dear Kum. Goel , Dear Smt. Gautam etc.

Sales/Circular Letters have salutations like 'Dear Customer', 'Dear Member', 'Dear Reader', 'Dear Subscriber' etc.

## 8. Subject (Place no 8 in the figure)

This line simply indicates what the letter is about therefore it should not exceed more than one line otherwise it would appear to be a letter inside a letter. The subject line is helpful in passing it to other / concerned departments if so required. It is typed in two spaces between the salutation and the main body. However some people prefer to type it between Attention Line and Salutation or between Inside Address and Salutation. Both the practices are correct however typing it between the salutation and the main body is better because greeting precedes every discussion.

## 9. Main Body (Place no 9 in the figure)

While writing the letter, it is always better to disclose your purpose of writing at the very first line. There should be no beating about the bushes. Come to the point directly. You can mention the reference number to any correspondence which has already taken place or to which you are responding. In that case, you needn't mention two reference numbers. Only the reference number of your letter is sufficient. Then you can mention the main message. You can mention further details in the following paragraphs / lines. The action expected from the reader should be mentioned in the closing paragraph / line or you can end the letter by expressing your wishes / expectations / intentions. You can divide the main body into different paragraphs depending upon the length of the main body and a change in the subject.

## 10. Complimentary Close (Place no 10 in the figure)

Complimentary close is a polite way of ending the letter or taking leave courteously. It is typed two spaces below the last line of the main body of the letter. The most common complimentary closes are 'Yours faithfully', 'Yours truly', and 'Yours sincerely' etc. The most common for business correspondence are 'Yours faithfully', 'Yours truly' and 'Your sincerely. 'Yours obediently' is especially for the Principal / Teachers. You may note here that no apostrophe comma has to be used with complimentary close. You may choose to write 'Faithfully yours' or 'Truly yours' also. If you find the above complimentary closes old fashioned, you may choose to write 'With best wishes' 'Best wishes' 'Regards' 'Kind regards' 'Best regards' etc. But 'Warm regards' 'Warm wishes' 'Warmly' are suitable for informal communication. They should not be used in formal communication like business correspondence. Think about your relation with the receiver of the letter and then decide.

## 11. Signature (Place no 11 in the figure)

The person who writes/replies the letter has to sign here. It is placed below the complimentary close. The name of the writer along with his designation is typed four spaces below the complimentary close providing sufficient space for the writer to sign here.( Remember, the assistant or the typist is not the writer of the letter. Writer here refers to the Head of the department or any employee who writes/replies the letter on behalf of the company.)

## 12. Identification Marks (Place no 12 in the figure)

It is like a secret code denoting the persons involved in the drafting of the letter. Generally, the initials of the names of the typist and the assistant are typed on the left margin e.g. if the assistant is Mr. Ravi Varma and The typist is Kusum Singh the identification may be written as:-

RV-KS

Or sometime only

KS

It indicates in the former case that the letter has been prepared by an assistant and a typist and in the latter case only the name of the typist is evident; perhaps the letter was dictated by the boss himself.

This mark is very necessary because it assigns responsibility of the typist and the assistant and in case of a mistake in the letter, it is possible to trace who committed it and it is helpful in taking suitable action. But you must remember that if you are writing your letter in complete block format, this element should occupy the last position or at the end of the letter. All elements should come before it.

## 13. Mailing Notation (Place no 13 in the figure).This notation states the method of mailing: whether the letter is sent registered, airmail, special delivery…etc. It is typed directly below the identification line or enclosure notation. It serves as a record to indicate that the letter was sent by other than regular mail.

## 14. Enclosure (Place no 14 in the figure)

If any document is attached with the letter, it is mentioned here as follows:-

Encl-2

Or

Enclosures-2

Or

Encls -1.   A copy of agreement (3Sep, 2003)
        2.   A cheque of Rs 400000 No. 346877 SBI Jabalpur

Or

Enclosures - 1. A copy of agreement (3Sep, 2003)
            2. A cheque of Rs 400000 No. 346877 SBI Jabalpur

## 15. CC: (Carbon Copy or Courtesy Copy) (Place no 15 in the figure)

If you are sending one or more copies of your letter to other office bearers/Heads of Departments, you need to mention all of them here as follows:-

Copy to 1. The Chief Minister of MP
        2. The Minister for Railways
        3. The Minister for Industries

The name CC: is abbreviation of Carbon Copy because earlier carbon copies of the letters were prepared if one or more copies of the letter were needed. Although carbon copy is no more in practice yet the name still exists in the form of abbreviation, CC. Presently CC: is known as Courtesy Copy also.

This notation states that a carbon copy of the letter is being sent to another person. It is typed two spaces below all other notation, flush with the left-hand margin. Either the word 'Copy to' or the abbreviation CC: may be used.

The blind carbon copy notation (bcc :) is used when the addresser does not wish to indicate the distribution of the carbon copies to the addressee. It appears on all internal copies, but not on the letter sent to the addressee.

## 16. Postscript

Postscript is used to write forgotten material after the letter has been finalized or finally printed. It may be hand written also. Sometimes it is written intentionally to attract the attention of the reader. But a good letter should not have a postscript because it does not reflect a good picture of the letter writer. Therefore, the content of the letter must include all the information so that nothing should be left for postscript.

## Punctuation of the letter

Nowadays letters are written with a minimum of the punctuation which is compulsory. All the unnecessary commas and full stops are avoided. This type of punctuation is known as Open Punctuation. In this style, no commas and full stops are used in any part of the letter except in the main body of the letter where usual punctuation marks are used.

The style of punctuation in which all the possible punctuation marks are used is known as Closed Punctuation whereas another style which is a compromise between the two, is known as Mixed Punctuation. In this style, the main body of the letter has usual punctuation marks and a comma is put after the date, the salutation and the complimentary close. A full stop is used after the inside address.

In Closed Punctuation every part of the letter is punctuated. The date, inside address, salutation and the complimentary close are punctuated as follows:-

Date: 14 May, 1997

Inside Address: Y.K. Akela,
                Managing Director,
Sangam Steel Company,
                45, Outer Ring Road,
                Gurgaon- (Haryana)-110033.

Salutation:    Dear Sir,
                    Or
                    Dear Sir:
Complimentary Close: Yours truly,
Out of these styles of punctuations, Mixed Style of punctuation is most popular. It's accepted most widely in the world.

# Other Important Points

## Stationary

The letter head must be printed on a good quality paper and the printing must be attractive enough to make a favorable impression. Nowadays many attractive designs of the letterhead are invented every year.

## Typing

The letters should be typed without any spelling or grammatical mistakes because the letters determine the initial impression. A little extra care will pay extra dividends. The letters must be crosschecked for errors before they are finalized. The fonts should neither be too small nor too big because small fonts are difficult to read and big fonts take extra space. At the final stage the fonts may be adjusted according to the availability of the space. Besides this, the fonts should be simple enough to be read by all. The complex types of fonts should be avoided for formal correspondence.

## Margin

To provide a balanced appearance or a picture frame appearance to the letter a proper margin should be left around it. For A4 size one inch on the left and right and half inch on the top and bottom is the standard margin. However the margin may be reduced for the smaller size letters.

## Envelope

Like the paper of the letter, the envelope should also be attractive and fitting to the size of the letter. It should have attractive printing and a neat appearance. For the window envelope, the letter should have such folds that the address is visible clearly with minimum number of folds.

# Various Styles of Presentation

Previously, you came to know of the two styles writing letters i.e. Block Style and Complete Block style. Letters may be written in various styles. Looking at the variety of styles, students are generally confused which is the correct style that they should adopt. In fact, the style is a personal choice as you already know. There is no question of its being correct or incorrect but its suitability certainly matters. Suitability too depends upon various factors.

At present, letters are written in the following styles:-

# 1. Complete Block Style / Full Block Format

All the parts of the letter are aligned with the left margin. This is the most convenient and time saving style but it appears imbalanced and loaded on the left side. In fact this style has been generated by the advent of computers. An exhibit of this type of letter is the following:-

# Complete Block Style

## Golden Eagle Freight Carriers Ltd.
### British Residency Mission Road
### Kolkata 330011 Phone- +91332657786, 87, 89

Ref-Adj-Fr-22

26 May 1999

Mrs. Pallavi Joshi
The Purchase Manager
Diamond Glassware Incorporation
Shahjahanpur Aligarh 478703

Dear Madam:

Subject: Your letter about damaged freight

I have just received your letter dated May 24 about the damaged shipment you received through Golden Eagle Freight and regret the inconvenience that it has caused to you.

From your account of the problem, I am quite sure that your request for Rs 2400 adjustment on the damage to the 2 crates of Yeti glasses will be granted. A certain amount of breakage of this sort is unavoidable in cross-country shipping; I am sorry that it was your company that had to be the one to suffer the delay.

Please keep the damaged crates in the same condition in which you received them until one of our representatives inspects them. That inspection should take place within 2 weeks.

If all is in order, as it sounds to be in your letter, you can expect the full reimbursement within 2 weeks after our representative's inspection.


Yours Sincerely,


Rakesh Kumar Shrivastava,

Customer Relations Officer
Golden Eagle Freight Carrier Ltd.
Kolkata 330011

R Ravi-PRoy

**Complete Block / Full Block Format Features**

1. All parts except the letter head are aligned with the left margin.
2. Open Punctuation

## 2. Block Style

This style is similar to the complete block style. The difference is that the date line, complimentary close and signature are aligned on the right side. Generally people use mixed punctuation for this style. An exhibit of this type of letter is the following:-

# Block Style

## Golden Eagle Freight Carriers Ltd.
### British Residency Mission Road
### Kolkata 330011 Phone- +91332657786, 87, 89

Ref-Adj-Fr-22                                                          26 May 1999

Mrs. Pallavi Joshi
The Purchase Manager
Diamond Glassware Incorporation
Shahjahanpur Aligarh 478703

Dear Madam:

Subject: Your letter about damaged freight

I have just received your letter dated May 24 about the damaged shipment you received
through Golden Eagle Tree Freight and regret the inconvenience that it has caused to you.

From your account of the problem, I am quite sure that your request for Rs 2400
adjustment on the damage to the 2 crates of Yeti glasses will be granted. A certain amount
of breakage of this sort is unavoidable in cross-country shipping; I am sorry that it was
your company that had to be the one to suffer the delay.

Please keep the damaged crates in the same condition in which you received them until
one of our representatives inspects them. That inspection should take place within 2
weeks.

If all is in order, as it sounds to be in your letter, you can expect the full reimbursement
within 2 weeks after our representative's inspection.

Yours Sincerely,


R Ravi-PRoy                                            Rakesh Kumar Shrivastava,

                                                       Customer Relations Officer
                                                       Golden Eagle Freight Carrier Ltd.
                                                       Kolkata 330011

**Block Format Features**

1. Date line, the complimentary close, and the signature are aligned with the right margin.

2. All other parts, except the letter head, are set flush left.

3. Two spaces between each unit and a single space within the unit.

3. Mixed Punctuation

# 3. Semi Block Style

This style is similar to block style. The difference is that the paragraphs of the letter are indented. Mixed punctation is found good for this style. An exhibit of this type of letter is the following:-

# Golden Eagle Freight Carriers Ltd.
## British Residency Mission Road
### Kolkata 330011 Phone- +91332657786, 87, 89

Ref-Adj-Fr-22                                             26 May 1999

Mrs. Pallavi Joshi
The Purchase Manager
Diamond Glassware Incorporation
Shahjahanpur Aligarh 478703

Dear Madam:

Subject: Your letter about damaged freight

I have just received your letter dated May 24 about the damaged shipment you received through Golden Eagle Freight and regret the inconvenience that it has caused to you.

From your account of the problem, I am quite sure that your request for Rs 2400 adjustment on the damage to the 2 crates of Yeti glasses will be granted. A certain amount of breakage of this sort is unavoidable in cross-country shipping; I am sorry that it was your company that had to be the one to suffer the delay.

Please keep the damaged crates in the same condition in which you received them until one of our representatives inspects them. That inspection should take place within 2 weeks.

If all is in order, as it sounds to be in your letter, you can expect the full reimbursement within 2 weeks after our representative's inspection.

Yours Sincerely,


R Ravi-PRoy                          Rakesh Kumar Shrivastava,

                                     Customer Relations Officer
                                     Golden Eagle Freight Carrier Ltd.
                                     Kolkata 330011

## Semi-block Format Features

1. Similar to block style.
2. The date, complimentary closing, and identification line start at the center.
3. Paragraphs are indented and all other lines start at the left margin.
3. Most general practice is to indent 10 spaces.
4. Many typists let the salutation govern the spaces in the indention. For instance, if the salutation and the name of the individual whom the letter is addressed to occupy 20 spaces, the space in the indention will be 20 spaces.
5. Mixed Punctuation.

# 4. Modified Block Style

This style is a modified version of semi-block style. Date line, the complimentary close, and the signature shift slightly right of the center of the page aligned at their left margin. Paragraphs are indented but not according to the salutation. An exhibit of this type of letter is the following:-

# Modified-Block Style

## Golden Eagle Freight Carriers Ltd.
### British Residency Mission Road
#### Kolkata 330011 Phone- +91332657786, 87, 89

Ref-Adj-Fr-22                                               26 May 1999

Mrs. Pallavi Joshi
The Purchase Manager
Diamond Glassware Incorporation
Shahjahanpur Aligarh 478703

Dear Madam:

Subject: Your letter about damaged freight

    I have just received your letter dated May 24 about the damaged shipment you received through Golden Eagle Freight and regret the inconvenience that it has caused to you.

    From your account of the problem, I am quite sure that your request for Rs 2400 adjustment on the damage to the 2 crates of Yeti glasses will be granted. A certain amount of breakage of this sort is unavoidable in cross-country shipping; I am sorry that it was your company that had to be the one to suffer the delay.

    Please keep the damaged crates in the same condition in which you received them until one of our representatives can inspect them. That inspection should take place within 2 weeks.

    If all is in order, as it sounds to be in your letter, you can expect the full reimbursement within 2 weeks after our representative's inspection.

Yours Sincerely,

R Ravi-PRoy                              Rakesh Kumar Shrivastava,

                                         Customer Relations Officer
                                         Golden Eagle Freight Carrier Ltd.
                                         Kolkata 330011

## Modified block Format Features

1. Similar to block style.
2. Date line, the complimentary close, and the signature remain slightly right of the center of the page aligned at their left margin.
3. Paragraphs indented.
4. Open punctuation.

# 5. Mixed Block Style

This style is similar to the complete block style written in open punctuation. Paragraphs are not indented. Date line, the complimentary close, and the signature begin at the center of the page aligned at their left margin. An exhibit of this type of letter is the following:-

# Mixed-Block Style

## Golden Eagle Freight Carriers Ltd.
### British Residency Mission Road
#### Kolkata 330011 Phone- +91332657786, 87, 89

Ref-Adj-Fr-22                                              26 May 1999

Mrs. Pallavi Joshi
The Purchase Manager
Diamond Glassware Incorporation
Shahjahanpur Aligarh 478703

Dear Madam:

Subject: Your letter about damaged freight

I have just received your letter dated May 24 about the damaged shipment you received
through Golden Eagle Freight and regret the inconvenience that it has caused to you.

From your account of the problem, I am quite sure that your request for Rs 2400
adjustment on the damage to the 2 crates of Yeti glasses will be granted. A certain amount
of breakage of this sort is unavoidable in cross-country shipping; I am sorry that it was
your company that had to be the one to suffer the delay.

Please keep the damaged crates in the same condition in which you received them until
one of our representatives inspects them. That inspection should take place within 2
weeks.

If all is in order, as it sounds to be in your letter, you can expect the full reimbursement
within 2 weeks after our representative's inspection.

                                              Yours Sincerely,




R Ravi-PRoy                                   Rakesh Kumar Shrivastava,

                                              Customer Relations Officer
                                              Golden Eagle Freight Carrier Ltd.
                                              Kolkata 330011

**Mixed Block Format Features**

1. Similar to complete block style.
2. Date line, the complimentary close, and the signature begin at the center of the page aligned at their left margin.
3. Paragraphs not indented.
4. Open Punctuation.

# 6. Indented Style

This is a very old style of business letter. Each new element is indented two to four spaces and it is written in closed punctuation. But it requires extra time and energy. An exhibit of this type of letter is the following:-

# Indented Style

## Golden Eagle Freight Carriers Ltd.
### British Residency Mission Road
#### Kolkata 330011 Phone- +91332657786, 87, 89

Ref-Adj-Fr-22                                                                 26 May 1999

Mrs. Pallavi Joshi
    The Purchase Manager
        Diamond Glassware Incorporation
            Shahjahanpur  Aligarh  478703

Dear Madam:

Subject: Your letter about damaged freight

    I have just received your letter dated May 24 about the damaged shipment you received through Golden Eagle Freight and regret the inconvenience that it has caused to you.

    From your account of the problem, I am quite sure that your request for Rs 2400 adjustment on the damage to the 2 crates of Yeti glasses will be granted. A certain amount of breakage of this sort is unavoidable in cross-country shipping; I am sorry that it was your company that had to be the one to suffer the delay.

    Please keep the damaged crates in the same condition in which you received them until one of our representatives can inspect them. That inspection should take place within 2 weeks.

    If all is in order, as it sounds to be in your letter, you can expect the full reimbursement within 2 weeks after our representative's inspection.

                                 Yours Sincerely,

R Ravi-PRoy                                                        Rakesh Kumar Shrivastava,

                                 Customer Relations Officer
                                Golden Eagle Freight Carrier Ltd.
                                     Kolkata 330011

**Indented Style Format Features**

1. Oldest form of letter
2. Similar to block style.
3.Every line of the inside address is indented.
4. Each new element is indented two to four spaces.
3. Closed Punctuation

# 7. Semi-indented Style

This style is very much similar to indented style. The difference is that the inside address in this style is not indented. . An exhibit of this type of letter is the following:-

# Semi-Indented Style

## Golden Eagle Freight Carriers Ltd.
### British Residency Mission Road
### Kolkata 330011 Phone- +91332657786, 87, 89

Ref-Adj-Fr-22                                        26 May 1999

Mrs. Pallavi Joshi
The Purchase Manager
Diamond Glassware Incorporation
Shahjahanpur Aligarh 478703

Dear Madam:

Subject: Your letter about damaged freight

    I have just received your letter dated May 24 about the damaged shipment you received through Golden Eagle Freight and regret the inconvenience that it has caused to you.

    From your account of the problem, I am quite sure that your request for Rs 2400 adjustment on the damage to the 2 crates of Yeti glasses will be granted. A certain amount of breakage of this sort is unavoidable in cross-country shipping; I am sorry that it was your company that had to be the one to suffer the delay.

    Please keep the damaged crates in the same condition in which you received them until one of our representatives inspects them. That inspection should take place within 2 weeks.

    If all is in order, as it sounds to be in your letter, you can expect the full reimbursement within 2 weeks after our representative's inspection.

Yours Sincerely,

R Ravi-PRoy                                  Rakesh Kumar Shrivastava,

Customer Relations Officer
Golden Eagle Freight Carrier Ltd.
Kolkata 330011

**Semi-Indented Format Features**

1. Similar to indented style.
2. Inside address is not indented.
3. Each new element is indented two to four spaces.
4. Closed Punctuation.

# 8. Hanging Indented Style

In this style, the first line of each paragraph is aligned on the left while all other lines are indented four or five spaces. Since it has many indentations, it consumes more time in writing. An exhibit of this type of letter is the following: -

# Hanging-Indented Style

## Golden Eagle Freight Carriers Ltd.
### British Residency Mission Road
### Kolkata 330011 Phone- +91332657786, 87, 89

Ref-Adj-Fr-22                                                          26 May 1999

Mrs. Pallavi Joshi
The Purchase Manager
Diamond Glassware Incorporation
Shahjahanpur Aligarh 478703

Dear Madam:

Subject: Your letter about damaged freight

I have just received your letter dated May 24 about the damaged shipment you received
through Golden Eagle Freight and regret the inconvenience that it has caused to you.

From your account of the problem, I am quite sure that your request for Rs 2400
adjustment on the damage to the 2 crates of Yeti glasses will be granted. A certain
amount of breakage of this sort is unavoidable in cross-country shipping; I am sorry
that it was your company that had to be the one to suffer the delay.

Please keep the damaged crates in the same condition in which you received them until one
of our representatives inspects them. That inspection should take place within 2
weeks.

If all is in order, as it sounds to be in your letter, you can expect the full reimbursement
within 2 weeks after our representative's inspection.

Yours Sincerely,


R Ravi-PRoy                                          Rakesh Kumar Shrivastava,

                                                     Customer Relations Officer
                                                     Golden Eagle Freight Carrier Ltd.
                                                     Kolkata 330011

## Hanging Indented Format Features

1. Similar to block style.
2. First line of each paragraph is aligned with the left margin.
3. All other lines are indented four or five spaces.
4. Mixed punctuation or Open punctuation.
5. It is acceptable in sales letters.
6. This form is effective in attracting attention because of its different arrangement from the common letter arrangement.

# 9. Simplified Style

Too much workload in the world of work has extremely simplified the business letter and letters are written in a very simplified style. This style is known as simplified style. Salutation and complimentary close are not written in this type of letter. An exhibit of this type of letter is the following: -

# Simplified Style

## Golden Eagle Freight Carriers Ltd.
### British Residency Mission Road
#### Kolkata 330011 Phone- +91332657786, 87, 89

Ref-Adj-Fr-22                                                      26 May 1999

Mrs. Pallavi Joshi
The Purchase Manager
Diamond Glassware Incorporation
Shahjahanpur Aligarh 478703

Subject: Your letter about damaged freight

I have just received your letter dated May 24 about the damaged shipment you received through Golden Eagle Freight and regret the inconvenience that it has caused to you.

From your account of the problem, I am quite sure that your request for Rs 2400 adjustment on the damage to the 2 crates of Yeti glasses will be granted. A certain amount of breakage of this sort is unavoidable in cross-country shipping; I am sorry that it was your company that had to be the one to suffer the delay.

Please keep the damaged crates in the same condition in which you received them until one of our representatives inspects them. That inspection should take place within 2 weeks.

If all is in order, as it sounds to be in your letter, you can expect the full reimbursement within 2 weeks after our representative's inspection.


R Ravi-PRoy                                         Rakesh Kumar Shrivastava,

                                                    Customer Relations Officer
                                                    Golden Eagle Freight Carrier Ltd.
                                                    Kolkata 330011

# Language of a business letter

Business letters must be precise and concise. They must inform their content clearly with the least possible words. Business men are generally short of time so they prefer precise and clear language. On the other hand, come to the point directly. There should be no beating about the bush or long introductions. Use simple words which everyone can understand. Besides the above traits, the language should be polite and formal. Nonstandard words, slang and jargon should be strictly avoided.

We should always be careful about the spellings, grammar, and punctuation of the letter. All these things together will finally decide the overall impression. Block language should strictly be avoided. Business letters require writing in full sentences.

In no case the letters should be written in anger or with an attitude of revenge even when no fault lies on our part.

***

# <u>Inviting Quotation</u>

The letter, which invites prices of proposed purchase from supplying organizations, is called a letter inviting quotation. Firms, organizations have to carry out different types of purchases from time to time. The best practice is to invite quotations (prices/price list of goods / articles / machinery etc) from different manufacturers / firms / suppliers, and compare the price, quality, and then order for goods. This letter informs about a business to the prospective supplier and creates a healthy competition for supplying a quality product at reasonable price, which is greatly helpful to the organizations wishing to purchase items in bulk quantity.

## Sample Letter Inviting Quotation

**Subject Matter for the letter**

Assume that you are the Purchase Manager in Swastika Cement Ltd. Maihar Road Katni. Under an expansion plan of your company, you need some items of furniture for your new offices. Write a letter inviting quotation for furniture to Blossom Furniture Ltd MK Road Bandra Mumbai

**Answer:-**

# Swastika Cement Ltd.

**Maihar Road Katni (MP) 486002**
**Phones-07674-3035449, 50, 51,52,53,**
**Fax-07674-3035460, 61, 62,63,**
**E-mail – swastikacement@rediffmail.com**
**Visit us on www. swastikacement.com**

24 April, 2009


**Reference-P-Q-F-369**


**The Sales Manager**
**Blossom Furniture Ltd.**
**MK Road Bandra Mumbai**

220076

Dear Sir,

Subject – Requirement of quotation for furniture

We are a fast growing cement company with our state- of –the- art plant at Katni (MP), having a turnover of Rs 3000 crores annually.

Under an expansion plan, we are opening our new offices in North Indian cities. For these offices, we require office furniture in bulk quantity.

Please quote the prices of the following items of furniture:-

| SN | Item | Description | Quantity in units |
|---|---|---|---|
| 1 | Office Chair | Steel tubular frame, velvet cushioned with cotton and ply colour - black | 250 ( Two hundred and fifty |
| 2 | Stool | Steel tubular frame, velvet cushioned with cotton and ply colour - black | 250 ( Two hundred and fifty |

Please note that we have to finalize this deal by 31 May 2009 and you must be in a position to deliver the consignment by 30 June 2009 by an insured rail transport only.

We pay our suppliers by cheque or DD whatever they prefer. We do not accept the consignment other than insured rail transport.

Thanks,

Yours faithfully,

Ravi Sharma
The Purchase Manager

PSK-LV

***

Note- You have seen the above letter in Complete Block Style. Now you can view the same letter in Block Style on the next page.

# Swastika Cement Ltd

Maihar Road Katni (MP) 486002
Phones-07674-3035449, 50, 51, 52, 53,
Fax-07674-3035460, 61, 62, 63,
E-mail – swastikacement@rediffmail.com
Visit us on www. swastikacement.com

Reference-P-Q-F-369                                                24 April, 2009

**The Sales Manager**
**Blossom Furniture Ltd**
**MK Road Bandra Mumbai**
**220076**

Dear Sir,

Subject – Requirement of quotation for furniture

We are a fast growing cement company with our state- of –the- art plant at Katni (MP), having a turn over of Rs 3000 crores annually.
Under an expansion plan, we are opening our new offices in North Indian cities.
For these offices, we require office furniture in bulk quantity.
Please quote the prices of the following items of furniture:-

| SN | Item | Description | Quantity in units |
|---|---|---|---|
| 1 | Office Chair | Steel tubular frame, velvet cushioned with cotton and ply Colour-Black | 250 (Two hundred and fifty) |
| 2 | Stool | Steel tubular frame, velvet cushioned with cotton and ply Colour-Black | 250 (Two hundred and fifty) |

Please note that we have to finalize this deal 31 May, 2009 and you must be in a position to deliver the consignment by 30 June, 2009 by an insured rail transport only.
We pay our suppliers by cheque or DD whatever they prefer.
We do not accept the consignment other than insured rail transport.

Thanks,

PSK-LV                                                        Yours faithfully,


                                                       **Ravi Sharma**
                                               **The Purchase Manager**

**Tips for writing a letter Inviting Quotation**

The letter inviting quotation is a very important letter. By this letter, the company is able to invite many prospective suppliers for the item that it intends to purchase, compare the quality and prices and order the best quality at reasonable prices.

If you are writing a letter inviting quotation, keep the following points in your mind:-

1. State the quantity required using appropriate measurement unit e.g. units / litres / metres / kgs / tons etc.
2. Provide an appropriate technical description of the item required.
3. Mention the kind of transportation that you prefer for the delivery of consignment e.g. by road transport, or by rail transport or by an insured rail transport etc.
4. Ask for the mode of payment that the prospective supplier prefers or you mention your choice.
5. Ask for after sale service if applicable.
6. Ask for the guarantee / warranty / special discounts offered on the product.
7. If you are going to make a bulk purchase, do not forget to mention it.

***

# The letter Sending Quotation

The letter, which replies to a letter of quotation by sending a price list of the required items, is called a letter sending quotation. This letter is very important because our good will brings the opportunity knocking at our door and which must be exploited to the full and that is why it needs to be written very carefully.

# Sample Letter
# Reply to the letter Inviting Quotation

**Subject Matter for the letter**

Assume that you are the Sales Manager in Blossom Furniture Ltd MK Road Bandra Mumbai. You receive a letter inviting quotation from The Purchase Manager Swastika Cement Ltd Maihar Road Katni.for some items of office furniture. Write a letter sending quotation for furniture of their requirement.

**Answer:-**

# Blossom Furniture Ltd.
## MK Road Bandra Mumbai 220076
### Phones-022-2035439, 40, 41, 42, 43,
### Fax-022-2035450, 51, 52, 53,
### E-mail – blossomfurniture@yahoomail.com
### Visit us on www.blossomfurniture.com

30 April, 2009

**Your Reference-P-Q-F-369**
**Our Reference-S-Q-F-12009**

**The Purchase Manager**
**Swastika Cement Ltd.**
**Maihar Road Katni (MP) 486002**

**Dear Sir,**

Subject – Quotation for furniture

Thank you very much for your letter dated 24 April 2009 inviting quotation for some items of office furniture.
I quote the prices for the same as under: -

| SN | Item | Description | Price per unit |
|---|---|---|---|
| 1 | Office Chair | Steel tubular frame, velvet cushioned on the seat and back with 4 mm ply and cotton. colour - black | Rs 1000 =00 Rs (One thousand) |
| 2 | Stool | Steel tubular frame, velvet cushioned on the seat with 4mm ply and cotton. colour - black | Rs 400=00 Rs (Four hundred) |

Please note that we have quoted most reasonable prices because you intend to purchase the furniture in bulk quantity. However, you have yet another chance for getting a further discount in the prices. It is that presently we are giving a ten percent discount on all cash purchases. Therefore, if your order reaches us by 15 May, 2009, along with the DD of the full amount, we will give you a ten percent discount.
We have a huge ready stock of furniture with us and we can manage to deliver the consignment by 30 June, 2009 easily.
We always send our consignment by an insured rail transport only.
We accept DD's only.
Finally, I request you to have a look at our catalog, containing the latest range of our furniture, enclosed with this letter. If you find any item suitable for your needs, you can include it with your order.
Thanks,

Yours faithfully,


Mohan Sharma
The Sales Manager

**Encl. Catalog**

**RKD-SM**

***

**Note- You have seen the above letter in Complete Block Style. Now you can view the same letter in Block Style on the next page.**

# Blossom Furniture Ltd

MK Road Bandra Mumbai 220076
Phones-022-2035439, 40, 41, 42, 43,
Fax-022-2035450, 51, 52, 53,
E-mail – blossomfurniture@yahoomail.com
Visit us on www.blossomfurniture.com

Your Reference-P-Q-F-369
Our Reference-S-Q-F-12009

30 April, 2009

**The Purchase Manager**
**Swastika Cement Ltd**
**Maihar Road Katni (MP) 486002**

Dear Sir,

**Subject – Quotation for furniture**

Thank you very much for your letter dated 24 April 2009 inviting quotation for some items of office furniture.
I quote the prices for the same as under:-

| SN | Item | Description | Price per unit |
|----|------|-------------|----------------|
| 1 | Office Chair | Steel tubular frame, velvet cushioned on the seat and back  with cotton and 4 mm ply  Colour-Black | Rs 1000=00 (Rs one thousand) |
| 2 | Stool | Steel tubular frame, velvet cushioned on the seat with cotton and 4mm ply Colour-Black | Rs 400=00 (Rs four hundred) |

Please note that we have quoted most reasonable prices because you intend to purchase the furniture in bulk quantity. However, you have yet another chance for getting a further discount in the prices. It is that presently we are giving a ten percent discount on all cash purchases. Therefore, if your order reaches us by 15 May, 2009, along with the DD of full amount, we will give you ten percent discount.
We have a huge ready stock of furniture with us and we can manage to deliver the consignment by 30 June, 2009 easily.
We always send our consignment by an insured rail transport only.
We accept DD's only.
Finally, I request you to have a look at our catalogue, containing latest range of our furniture, enclosed with this letter. If you find any item suitable for your needs, you can include it with your order.

Thanks,

RKD-SM
Encl. Catalogue

Yours faithfully,

**Mohan Sharma**
**The Sales Manager**

## Tips for writing a letter sending Quotation

The letter which is written in reply to an invitation to quotation or it is a letter which sends the price list of the products which a purchaser proposes to purchase.

If you are writing a letter sending quotation,

1.  Be sure that you are giving the correct description and specification of the item/s.
2.  State the prices per unit / per kg / per liter / per meter / or per quintal as applicable.
3.  State the mode of payment, packing, and transportation besides the place and time of delivery.
4.  If the after sales service is required, mention the facilities you provide.
5.  Do mention the guarantee/ warranty that you provide on the product/s.
6.  Do not forget to mention the charges on account of sales tax, freight, insurance, packing and forwarding if applicable.

Remember that the letter sending quotation is very much similar to a sales letter therefore it must have the necessary sales punch required for a sales letter. You can take the following measures to ensure the inclusion of a sales punch in it.

1.  Mention and provide special discounts on bulk purchases.
2.  Mention and provide further discounts on cash purchases from time to time specially when the sales are low.
3.  Mention the special quality and benefits that your product is capable of providing.
4.  Mention the guarantee/ warranty that you provide and how it is different from others.
5.  Send a brochure / catalog of your products with your letter even when it is not asked and make a request for its perusal.

***

# <u>Placing the Order</u>

The letter that is written to place the order is called the letter placing the order.

The next important activity / letter after inviting quotation is to place the order. When you have received various quotations from different suppliers you have to make a decision in favor of the one, which is supplying the best quality for very reasonable prices. This letter is also very important or better to say the most important of the three because any mistake here may lead to a legal dispute. Therefore, once again you should write this letter very carefully.

# Sample Letter
# The letter placing the Order

**Subject Matter for the letter**

Assume that you are the Purchase Manager in Swastika Cement Ltd Maihar Road Katni.. You receive quotation for some items of office furniture from The Sales Manager Blossom Furniture Ltd MK Road Bandra Mumbai as per your request. You find that the quotation from Blossom Furniture Ltd MK Road Bandra Mumbai is the best and has the most reasonable prices.  Write a letter placing the order for furniture of your requirement.

**Answer:-**

# Swastika Cement Ltd.
## Maihar Road Katni (MP) 486002
## Phones-07674-3035449, 50, 51,52,53,
## Fax-07674-3035460, 61, 62,63,
### E-mail – swastikacement@rediffmail.com
### Visit us on swastikacement.com

**5 May, 2009**

**Your Reference-S-Q-F-12009**
**Our Reference – P – Ord - 25567**

**The Sales Manager**

**Blossom Furniture Ltd.**
**MK Road Bandra Mumbai**
**220076**

Dear Sir,

Subject – Order for furniture

Thank you very much for your letter dated 30 April 2009 offering quotation for some items of office furniture of our requirement.

We are pleased to inform you that your quotation has been found most reasonable.

I hereby place the order for the following items of office furniture:-

| SN | Item | Description | Quantity in units |
|---|---|---|---|
| 1 | Office Chair | Steel tubular frame, velvet cushioned on the seat and back with 4 mm ply and cotton. colour - black | 250 ( Two hundred and fifty |
| 2 | Stool | Steel tubular frame, velvet cushioned on the seat with 4mm ply and cotton. colour - black | 250 ( Two hundred and fifty |

We are sending a DD of Rs 315000=00 (three lakh fifteen thousand only) with this letter as full payment of the furniture. We have already deducted a 10 % cash purchase discount from the total price. We are sure that you shall receive this order well before 15 May 2009.

We hope that the delivery of the furniture will be complete well before 30 June. 2009.

Please send the furniture by an insured rail transport only.

Finally, I thank you for your catalog. Presently we require the above-mentioned furniture only. However, we will certainly order the piece that we find useful for our future use.

Thanks,

Yours faithfully,


Ravi Sharma
The Purchase Manager

A DD of Rs 315000=00
issued by SBI Katni
Dated  5 May, 2009

PSK-LV

***

**Note-** You have seen the above letter in Complete Block Style. Now you can view the same letter in Block Style on the next page.

# Swastika Cement Ltd

Maihar Road Katni (MP) 486002
Phones-07674-3035449, 50, 51,52,53,
Fax-07674-3035460, 61, 62,63,
E-mail – swastikacement@rediffmail.com
Visit us on swastikacement.com

Your Reference-S-Q-F-12009
Our Reference – P – Ord - 25567                                          5 May, 2009

**The Sales Manager**
**Blossom Furniture Ltd**
**MK Road Bandra Mumbai**
**220076**

Dear Sir,

Subject – Order for furniture

Thank you very much for your letter dated 30 April 2009 offering quotation for some items of office furniture of our requirement.
We are pleased to inform you that your quotation has been found most reasonable.
I hereby place the order for the following items of office furniture:-

| SN | Item | Description | Quantity in units |
|---|---|---|---|
| 1 | Office Chair | Steel tubular frame, velvet cushioned on the seat and back with cotton and 4 mm ply  Colour-Black | 250 (Two hundred and fifty) |
| 2 | Stool | Steel tubular frame, velvet cushioned on the seat with cotton and 4mm ply Colour-Black | 250 (Two hundred and fifty) |

We are sending a DD of Rs 315000=00 (three lakh fifteen thousand only) with this letter as full payment of the furniture. We have already deducted 10 % cash purchase discount from the total price. We are sure that you shall receive this order well before 15 May 2009.
We hope that the delivery of the furniture will be complete well before 30 June. 2009.
Please send the furniture by an insured rail transport only.
Finally, I thank you for your catalogue. Presently we require the above-mentioned furniture only. However, we will certainly order the piece that we find useful for our future use.
Thanks,

PSK-LV                                                              Yours faithfully,
Encl. A DD of Rs 315000=00
issued by SBI Katni
Dated 5 May, 2009

                                                                   Ravi Sharma

                                                          The Purchase Manager

## Tips for writing the letter placing the order

This letter must be written with great care because once you have placed the order; you cannot make any corrections. The mistakes in this letter are unpardonable and may land you in the court.

If you are writing a letter placing the order,

1.  Be sure that you are giving correct description and specification of the item/s

    It is preferable to use the description / specification sent by the supplier after checking that it is as per your requirement. No change in the specification / design is advisable at this stage. In case you need to make any changes, you must send your requirement to your supplier afresh and confirm that they can do it.

2.  State the quantity ordered per unit / per kg / per liter / per meter / or per quintal as applicable.( You can mention the quantity in words and figures both as an extra precaution)

3.  Mention the mode of payment, packing, and transportation besides the place and time of delivery once again in this letter.

4.  Do mention the number and amount of the DD / Cheque along with its date and the name and address of the issuing bank, which you are sending with the letter.

5.  Mention once again the deadline for the supply of the consignment if any.

***

# The Letter of Claim or complaint

The letter of claim or complaint is written with a view to complaining about any problem with the product that you have purchased from a supplier and getting suitable compensation for the loss if any or getting the product repaired or corrected. E.g., you have purchased a machine / equipment from a supplier / company but it started malfunctioning after six months although the machine / equipment is supported by a one year guarantee. Or you have received a short supply / wrong supply (a product not required/ordered). Alternatively, the product that you have received is not functioning properly. Similarly, it may have some manufacturing defects and so on. All such situations make a subject for the letter of claim or complaint.

This letter is very sensitive and needs to be written tactfully so that the supplier may not be offended and we are able to get a suitable compensation.

# Sample Letter
# The letter of Claim or Complaint

**Subject Matter for the letter**

Assume that you are the Purchase Manager in Swastika Cement Ltd  Maihar Road Katni (MP).. You placed an order for some pieces of furniture, with Maswyne Furniture Ltd. MK Road Bandra Mumbai. But you have received the furniture nonconforming to the quality required by you and the quality promised by Maswyne Furniture Ltd.  Write a letter of complaint.

**Answer:-**

# Swastika Cement Ltd.
### Maihar Road Katni (MP) 486002
### Phones-07674-3035449, 50, 51,52,53,

Fax-07674-3035460, 61, 62,63,

E-mail – swastikacement@rediffmail.com

Visit us on swastikacement.com

15 May, 2009

Reference – P – Cl – 431

**The Sales Manager**
**Maswyne Furniture Ltd.**
**MK Road Bandra Mumbai**
**220076**

**Dear Sir,**

**Subject – Complaint about poor quality furniture**

I regret to inform you that the office chairs sent by you (Invoice Number- OF – 23654) as per our order dated 5May, 2009 (Ref-P-Ord-25567 Item 4) have been found made of poor quality material nonconforming to our requirement and the quotation sent by you (Ref.-S-Q-F-12009).

As per our requirement and the quotation sent by you, these chairs should have been stuffed with cotton but they have been found stuffed with waste material of cloth and foam.(Please see the certificate issued by our Store Manager enclosed with this letter.)

I do not think that you have intentionally cheated us but it might be a mistake also.

I request you to inquire into the matter and replace these chairs with the chairs of our requirement.

I am sure that our grievances shall be listened to and provided for.

Thanks,

Yours faithfully,

Ravi Sharma
The Purchase Manager

Encl. A copy of certificate
      issued by our store manager.

PSK-LV

***

**Note- You have seen the above letter in Complete Block Style. Now you can view the same letter in Block Style on the next page.**

# Swastika Cement Ltd

Maihar Road Katni (MP) 486002
Phones-07674-3035449, 50, 51,52,53,
Fax-07674-3035460, 61, 62,63,
E-mail – swastikacement@rediffmail.com
Visit us on swastikacement.com

Reference – P – Cl – 431          15 May, 2009

The Sales Manager
Maswyne Furniture Ltd
MKRoad Bandra Mumbai
220076

Dear Sir,

Subject – Complaint about poor quality furniture

I regret to inform you that the office chairs sent by you (Invoice Number- OF – 23654) as per our order dated 5 May, 2009 (Ref-P-Ord-25567 Item 1) have been found made of poor quality material nonconforming to our requirement and the quotation sent by you (Ref.-S-Q-F-12009).

As per our requirement and the quotation sent by you, these chairs should have been stuffed with cotton but they have been found stuffed with waste material of cloth and foam.(Please see the certificate issued by our Store Manager enclosed with this letter.)

I do not think that you have intentionally cheated us but it might be a mistake also.

I request you to enquire into the matter and replace these chairs with the chairs of our requirement.

I am sure that our grievances shall be listened to and provided for.

Thanks,

PSK-LV

                 Yours faithfully,

Encl. A copy of certificate
     issued by our store manager.

                 Ravi Sharma
                 The Purchase Manager

# Tips for writing a letter of claim or complaint

A letter of complaint is a very sensitive letter. Therefore, it needs a balanced mind and tactful handling.

Keep the following points in your mind while writing this letter:-

**(i)** Since the letter of complaint is a sensitive letter and the sufferer tends to be angry, there are great chances that the anger and frustration may be reflected in the letter of complaint therefore it is advisable that you keep your mind cool and calm while writing this letter. An angry tone will only worsen the situation.

**(ii)** Don't leave the usual courtesy and politeness even in the extreme situations. Politeness and courtesy will help to set the things right however worse the case may be

**(iii)** Even when you know clearly that the loss / damage has occurred due to the fault by the party being addressed, you should not blame anyone directly and your language must be polite. It must not break the boundaries of civility and politeness

**(iv)** You can give the suspected cause or person behind the loss or fault politely.

**(v)** Don't resort to an abusive language. This is strictly forbidden.

**(vi)** Don't blame anyone directly. Simply state in clear language what has gone wrong, the nature and extent of damage and further loss suffered due to it.

**(vii)** Mention the order number, invoice number with date of purchase / order, model number / make etc whichever applicable.

**(viii)** Mention clearly the guarantee / warranty / after sales service offered against it.

**(ix)** Don't exaggerate the loss / damage. The letter of complaint must contain the real state of affairs.

**(x)** The letter must be supported by a certificate from the store manager or the inspecting authority.

**(xi)** An appeal of fair play, honesty, or goodwill will work better and it will provide a greater motivation for the rectification of the error or proper adjustment.

***

# Adjustment Letter

The letter, which replies the letter of claim or complaint, is termed as Adjustment Letter. This letter does not necessarily mean making financial adjustments as the name indicates. It is simply a reply to a letter of complaint with or without financial adjustment. This letter again like a letter of complaint is a letter dealing with a sensitive matter and therefore like a letter of complaint, this letter also requires tactful handling and a balanced and polite reply.

However, you have either to provide a suitable compensation through this letter or simply inform the audience that no liability lies on our side for the damage because it has been caused due to improper handling by the operator or during transportation by the transporter.

Keep the following points in your mind while writing this letter:-

**(i)** Since the complainer has suffered a loss, the anger and frustration are natural; you need to be polite, balanced, submissive, calm and avoid reaction from your side.

**(ii)** Don't pay the writer of the letter in the same coin even when his language is abusive, harsh or he has resorted to the angry tone. Writing discourteous, abusive, or angry letters will cost you the loss of goodwill and business both. It always pays to be courteous in business. Send a courteous and polite reply and, in all probability, the other person will respond more favorably.

**(iii)** Adopt a sympathetic attitude towards the complainer even when you know that the complainer himself is at fault or the loss occurred due to his own negligence. Express your concern for the loss, tell the possible causes of the loss and advise him politely what to do next and how to avoid such damages.

**(iv)** If the damage can be compensated by an insurance company, provide full support in this regard e.g. the address of the insurance company, relevant information and documental support.

**(v)** If the damage has occurred due to the fault on your side, accept it politely. Provide a suitable compensation and thank / express gratitude to the letter writer for informing you about your shortcoming that could have damaged the goodwill of the company. Besides this, make a promise not to repeat it again.

# Sample Letter
# Adjustment Letter

**Subject Matter for the letter**

Assume that you are the Sales Manager in Maswyne Furniture Ltd. MK Road Bandra Mumbai 220076. You receive a letter of complaint from Sawastika Cement  Ltd Maihar Road Katni (MP) saying that they have received poor quality furniture nonconforming to the quality required by you and the quality promised by you. Write a letter of Adjustment.

**Answer:-**

# Maswyne Furniture Ltd.
**MK Road Bandra Mumbai 220076**
**Phones-022-2035439, 40, 41, 42, 43,**
**Fax-022-2035450, 51, 52, 53,**
**E-mail – alwynefurniture@yahoomail.com**
**Visit us on alwynefurniture.com**

5June, 2009

**Your Reference-P-Cl-431**
**Our Reference-S-Adj-12**

**The Purchase Manager**
**Swastika Cement Ltd.**
**Maihar Road Katni (MP) 486002**

**Dear Sir,**

Subject – Adjustment against the supply of nonconforming quality of furniture:

I am very much sorry to note that you have received the nonconforming quality of office chairs. I regret the inconvenience caused due to this mistake from our side. However, I assure you that everything will be alright very soon. We will take back the nonconforming office chairs and send you the office chairs of your requirements.
I request you to contact our local agent at the following contact information:-
Rachna Furnishers
24 Adarsha Nagar Satna (MP)
585001
Phones- 07672-430876- M- 9887654034
We have sent them instructions in this regard. They will cooperate with you. They have sufficient stock of the office chairs required by you. Please return all the office chairs not required by you. The vehicle from the Rachna Furnishers will do all the transportation.
I thank you very much for your cooperation and for informing us in time. Please feel free to inform us of the further troubles if you encounter any in our further dealings. I promise you that no such incident shall ever take place in future again.

Thanks,


Yours faithfully,

Ravi Sharma
The Purchase Manager

RKD-SM

***

**Note- You have seen the above letter in Complete Block Style. Now you can view the same letter in Block Style on the next page.**

# Maswyne Furniture Ltd

MK Road Bandra Mumbai 220076
Phones-022-2035439, 40, 41, 42, 43,
Fax-022-2035450, 51, 52, 53,
E-mail – alwynefurniture@yahoomail.com
Visit us on alwynefurniture.com

Your Reference-P-Cl-431
Our Reference-S-Adj-12                                         5 June, 2009

The Purchase Manager
Swastika Cement Ltd
Maihar Road Katni (MP) 486002

Dear Sir,

Subject – Adjustment against the supply of nonconforming quality of furniture:

I am very much sorry to note that you have received the nonconforming quality of office chairs. I regret the inconvenience caused due to this mistake from our side. However, I assure you that everything will be all right very soon. We will take back the nonconforming office chairs and send you the office chairs of your requirements.
I request you to contact our local agent at the following contact information. :-
Rachna Furnishers
24 Adarsha Nagar Satna (MP)
585001
Phones- 07672-430876- M- 9887654034
We have sent them instructions in this regard. They will cooperate with you. They have sufficient stock of the office chairs required by you. Please return them all the office chairs not required by you. The vehicle from the Rachna Furnishers will do all the transportation.
I thank you very much for your cooperation and for informing us in time. Please feel free to inform us of the further troubles if you encounter any in our further dealings.
I promise you that no such incident shall ever take place in future again.
Thanks,
RKD-SM                                                  Yours faithfully,


                                                        Ravi Sharma
                                                        The Purchase Manager

# The Letter of Inquiry

The letter of inquiry is very much similar to the letter inviting quotation. The difference between the two lies in their purpose. The letter inviting quotation seeks the prices of the items / goods that you intend to purchase but the letter of inquiry seeks information on any sort of matter. It is not necessary that this letter cannot invite quotation but besides seeking information, quotations may also be invited if it is required. This letter may seek any general information except that it is not confidential and the company, which has to part with some information, will not suffer any loss by giving the required information.

Keep the following points in your mind while writing this letter:-

**(i)** Remember that companies part with some information out of good will. No liability for giving such information lies on their shoulders. Therefore, you need to be polite enough while asking for any information.

**(ii)** You have to be polite, appropriate, precise and concise while writing this letter similarly like the letter inviting quotation.

**(iii)** Provide appropriate data and technical description if the need be.

**(iv)** If you are writing a letter to a company for the first time, provide a small introduction of your company in the beginning and come to the point very soon.

# Sample Letter
# Letter of Inquiry

**Subject Matter for the letter**

Assume that you are the Purchase Manager in Kay Pee Constructions Pvt. Ltd. Sarita Complex Third Storey near Sarai Kale Khan Faridabad (UP) NCR .  You have some old tractors from Schwing Stetter, a company of German Origin These tractors are working nicely except that their diesel pumps have developed some problems and they need to be replaced. Write a letter of inquiry to Ortem Diesel Pumps Ltd 23 Vision Towers MG Road Pune asking them if they can manufacture the diesel pumps of your requirement.

**Answer:-**

# Kay Pee Constructions Pvt. Ltd.

**Sarita Complex, Third Storey, near Sarai Kale Khan
Faridabad (UP) NCR 110029
Phones-011-23435429, 30,31,32,33,
Fax-011-23435470, 71, 72,73
Email – kpconstructions@rediffmail.com
Visit us on kpconstructios.com**

**15 April, 2009**

**Reference- P – Inq - 46**

## The Sales Manager

**Ortem Diesel Pumps Ltd.
23 Vision Towers
MG Road Pune -  440099**

**Dear Sir,**

**Subject – Inquiry.**

**We are a construction company engaged in the construction of dams and housing colonies, having our strong presence in India since 1949.**

We have 25 tractors of 45 horse power from Schwing Stetter, a German Company. These tractors are now thirty years old and they have developed problems with their diesel pumps. At present these pumps must be replaced with new diesel pumps. These diesel pumps are available with the company but their cost is too heavy. But if someone can manufacture them here in India, they will be pretty cheap for us.

I am sending the design and technical specifications of the diesel pump. Please see it and if you can manufacture them, I request you to send the quotation of 30 such pumps.

I am quite hopeful that you will be able to manufacture them and avail them to us at reasonable prices.

Thanks,

Yours faithfully,


Rakesh Mishra
The Purchase Manager

Encl- Design and Technical
Description of Diesel pump

RPM-LS

***


Note- You have seen the above letter in Complete Block Style. Now you can view the same letter in Block Style on the next page.

# Kay Pee Constructions Pvt. Ltd

**Sarita Complex ,Third Storey, near Sarai Kale Khan**
**Faridabad (UP) NCR 110029**
**Phones-011-23435429, 30,31,32,33, Fax-011-23435470, 71, 72,73**
**E-mail – kpconstructions@rediffmail.com**
**Visit us on kpconstructios.com**

Reference- P – Inq - 46                                                15 April, 2009

The Sales Manager
Ortem Diesel Pumps Ltd
23 Vision Towers
MG Road Pune -  440099

Dear Sir,

Subject – Inquiry.

We are a construction company engaged in the construction of dams and housing
colonies, having our  strong presence in India since 1949.
We have 25 tractors of 45 horse power  from Schwing Stetter, a German Company.
These tractors are now thirty years old and they have developed problems with
their diesel pumps. At present these pumps must be replaced with new diesel
pumps. These diesel pumps are available with the company but their cost is too
heavy. But if someone can manufacture them here in India, they will be pretty
cheap for us.
I am sending the design and technical specifications of the diesel pump. Please see
it and if you can manufacture them,
I request you to send the quotation of 30 such pumps.
I am quite hopeful that you will be able to manufacture them and avail them to us
at reasonable prices.
Thanks,

RPM-LS                                                               Yours faithfully,
Encl- Design and Technical
Description of Diesel pump


                                                               Rakesh Mishra
                                                               The Purchase Manager

# More Business letters

**Q1.** You are Ramesh Khurana the Purchase Manager in Ultramodern Cables Ltd. Industrial Area Chorahata Rewa (MP) Write a letter to Hindustan Computers Ltd. 35 Arera Complex Industrial Area Greater Noida (UP) inviting quotation for 30 computers for your organization.

**Ans.**

# Ultramodern Cables Ltd.

### Industrial Area,Chorahata Rewa (MP)
**Phones-07662-23435429, 30,31,32,33, Fax-07662-23435480, 81, 82,83**

**Email – ultramoderncables@rediffmail.com**
**Visit us on ultramoderncable.com**

15 April, 2003


Reference- P – Quo - 23


**The Sales Manager**
**Hindustan Computers Ltd.**
**35 Arera Complex**
**Greater Noida (UP) 110001**


Dear Sir,


Subject – Requirement of quotation.


We are an ISO 9001-2000 certified cable manufacturing company, having our strong presence in MP since 1980.

We have computerized the whole process of cable manufacturing. We have already purchased 200 computers from you and I am pleased to mention that these computers are working very nicely. Now we need to purchase 30 more for our packing section as per specifications mentioned below.

| SN | Item | Description | Quantity Required |
|---|---|---|---|
| 1 | CPU Desktop | Intel- P5, Core to Quod, WiFi ready<br>320 GB HDD, DVD Writer, 1 GB RAM | 30 units<br>(Thirty units) |
| 2 | Multimedia Keyboard | Multimedia Keyboard with all function keys<br>TVS Gold Super | 30 units<br>(Thirty units) |
| 3 | Optical Mouse | Optical Mouse with USB Port | 30 units<br>(Thirty units) |
| 4 | TFT Monitor | TFT Monitor with inbuilt speakers, 19 inches | 30 units<br>(Thirty units) |
| 5 | UPS | 5KVA UPS System with Exide Batteries | 3 Assemblies (Three Assemblies) |

I request you to send the quotation for above-mentioned items.

Here I need to mention that we have to finalize this deal by 15 June 2003 and we must get our consignment by 30 June 2003. Thus you should be in a position to supply our consignment by this date.

But I am sure that you have sufficient ready stock to meet our demand..

Thanks,

Yours truly,


Ramesh Khurana
The Purchase Manager

RPM-M S

***

## Response to the above letter
# <u>The Letter Sending Quotation</u>

# Hindustan Computers Ltd.

## 35 Arera Complex Greater Noida (UP) 110001
### Phones-012-23435429, 30,31,32,33, Fax-012-234354650, 51, 52,53
### E-mail – hindustancomputers@rediffmail.com
### Visit us on hindustancomputers.com

20 April, 2003


Your Reference- P – Quo – 23
Our Reference- S – Q - 34527


## The Purchase Manager
**Ultramodern Cables Ltd.**
**Industrial Area,Chorahata Rewa (MP)**
**484009**


Dear Sir,


Subject – quotation.


Thank you very much for your letter seeking quotation for desktop computer systems and UPS systems for your organization.

I hereby quote the prices of the desktop computer systems and UPS systems as per your requirement:-

| SN | Item | Description | Price per Unit |
|---|---|---|---|
| 1 | CPU Desktop | Intel- P5, Core to Quod, WiFi ready 320 GB HDD, DVD Writer, 1 GB RAM | Rs 12000 |
| 2 | Multimedia Keyboard | Multimedia Keyboard with all function keys TVS Gold Super | Rs 1000 |
| 3 | Optical Mouse | Optical Mouse with USB Port | Rs 300 |
| 4 | TFT Monitor | TFT Monitor with inbuilt speakers, 19 inches | Rs 9000 |
| 5 | UPS Assembly | 5KVA UPS System with two Exide Batteries | Rs 30000 |
| 6 | Transportation Charges | For all the 30 desktop computer systems and three UPS system Assemblies | Rs 6000 |

We have quoted most reasonable rates because you are our old and valuable customer.

We have sufficient ready stock to meet your requirements. We will dispatch the consignment by an insured rail transport as soon as we get your order.

Please send the order before 15 May 2003. If we get your order with full payment of the computers on or before 15 May 2003, you shall get these computers without paying for the transportation charges.

Thank you very much,

Regards,


Rajesh  Shrivastava
The Sales Manager

CPM-V S

***

**Q2.** You are Mahesh Varma the Purchase Manager in Kay Pee Constructions Pvt. Ltd. Sarita Complex Third Storey near Sarai Kale Khan Faridabad (UP) NCR . Write a letter to Hexon Pumps Pvt. Ltd. 35 SR Complex Industrial Area Adyar Chennai Tamil Nadu inviting quotation for 100 water pumps for your housing colonies.

**Ans.**

# Kay Pee Constructions Pvt. Ltd.

**Sarita Complex, Third Storey, near Sarai Kale Khan
Faridabad (UP) NCR 110029**
**Phones-011-23435429, 30,31,32,33, Fax-011-23435440, 41, 42,43**
**Email – kpconstructions@rediffmail.com**
**Visit us on kpconstructios.com**

15 April, 2003
Reference- P – Q - 59


**The Sales Manager**

Hexon Pumps Pvt. Ltd.
35 SR Complex
Industrial Area Adyar
Chennai Tamil Nadu - 440099

Dear Sir,

Subject – Requirement of quotation.

We are a construction company engaged in the construction of dams and housing colonies, having our strong presence in India since 1949.

We require one hundred units of half horsepower water pumps for our housing colonies for water pumping purpose for individual flats as per the following specifications:-

| SN | Item | Description | Quantity Required |
|---|---|---|---|
| 1 | Water pump | Half Horse Power, inlet = half inch, outlet = half inch | 100 units |
| | | RPM = Ranging between 1000 to 1500, Self priming | (one hundred units) |

Please quote the prices for the above mentioned water pumps. Please note that we have to finalize this deal by 15 May 2003. Besides this, you must be in a position to deliver the consignment well before 30 June 2003.
We pay our customers by cheque or DD whatever they wish. We accept the consignment by an insured rail transport only.
Thanks,

With best wishes,


Mahesh Varma
The Purchase Manager

RCM-VS

***

## Response to the above letter
## <u>The Letter Sending Quotation</u>

# Hexon Pumps Pvt. Ltd.
### 35 SR Complex Industrial Area Adyar
### Chennai Tamil Nadu -  440099
### Phones-044-23435429, 30,31,32,33, Fax-044-23435450, 51
### E-mail – exonpumps@yahoomail.com
### Visit us on exonpumps.com

25 April, 2003

Your Reference- P – Q - 59
Our Reference- S – Q - 12768

## The Purchase Manager
**Kay Pee Constructions Pvt. Ltd.**
**Sarita Complex ,Third Storey, near Sarai Kale Khan**
**Faridabad (UP) NCR 110029**

Dear Sir,

Subject – Quotation for water pumps

Thank you very much for your letter dated 15 April 2003 seeking quotation for water pumps for your housing colonies.
I hereby quote the prices of the water pumps of your requirement:-

| SN | Item | Description | Price per unit |
|---|---|---|---|
| 1 | Varuna | Half Horse Power, inlet = half inch, outlet = half inch, | Rs 3000=00 |
| | Water pump | 1500,RPM and self priming | (Rs three thousand only) |

We have quoted most reasonable rates because you are purchasing the pumps in bulk quantity.

We have sufficient ready stock to meet your requirements. We will dispatch the consignment by an insured rail transport as soon as we get your order.

Please send the order through a DD before 15 May 2003. If we get your order for pumps with full payment on or before 30 May 2003, you shall get these pumps without paying for the transportation charges.

Please look at the catalog of the latest range of our water pumps enclosed with this letter and if you wish to purchase any of them, you can include them with your order.

Thanks,

Kind regards,


Rajeev Ranjan
The Purchase Manager

Encl. Catalog

RCM-VS

***

# Placing The Order
## Some more letters

# <u>Placing the Order for Desktop Computers</u>

# Ultramodern Cables Ltd.

## Industrial Area,Chorahata Rewa (MP)
**Phones-07662-23435429, 30,31,32,33, Fax-07662-23435460, 61, 62,63,4**
**E-mail – ultramoderncables@rediffmail.com**
**Visit us on ultramoderncable.com**

30 April, 2003

Your Reference- S – Q - 34527
Our Reference- P – Ord - 23

**The Sales Manager**
**Hindustan Computers Ltd.**
**35 Arera Complex**
**Greater Noida (UP) 110001**

Dear Sir,

Subject – Order for Desktop Computers.

Thank you very much for your letter dated 20 April 2003 offering quotation for the desktop computers of our requirement.

We are pleased to inform you that your quotation has been found most reasonable.

I hereby place the order for the following items of our requirement:-

| SN | Item | Description | Quantity Required |
|---|---|---|---|
| 1 | CPU Desktop | Intel- P5, Core to Quod, WiFi ready | 30 units |
| | | 320 GB HDD, DVD Writer, 1 GB RAM | (Thirty units) |
| 2 | Multimedia Keyboard | Multimedia Keyboard with all function keys | 30 units |
| | | TVS Gold Super | (Thirty units) |
| 3 | Optical Mouse | Optical Mouse with USB Port | 30 units |
| | | | (Thirty units) |
| 4 | TFT Monitor | TFT Monitor with inbuilt speakers, 19 inches | 30 units |
| | | | (Thirty units) |
| 5 | UPS | 5KVA UPS System with Exide Batteries | 3 Assemblies (Three Assemblies) |

We are sending a DD of Rs 528750=00 (five lakh twenty eight thousand seven hundred and fifty) with this letter as full payment of the computers and the accessories. We are sure that you shall receive this order well before 15 May 2003.

We hope that the delivery of the systems will be complete well before 30 June. 2003.

Please send the systems properly packed in damage proof cartoons by an insured rail transport only.

Thanks,

Yours faithfully,


Mahesh Varma
The Purchase Manager


Encl. A DD of Rs 528750=00
issued by SBI Katni
Dated  29 April,2003


RSK-LT

***

# Placing the Order for water Pumps

# Kay Pee Constructions Pvt. Ltd.

## Sarita Complex ,Third Storey, near Sarai Kale Khan
## Faridabad (UP) NCR 110029
Phones-011-23435429, 30,31,32,33,Fax-011-23435470, 71, 72,73
Email –kpconstructions@rediffmail.com
Visit us on kpconstructios.com

15 April, 2003

Your Reference- S – Q - 12768
Our Reference- P – Ord - 45659

## The Sales Manager

**Hexon Pumps Pvt. Ltd.**
**35 SR Complex**
**Industrial Area Adyar**
**Chennai Tamil Nadu -  440099**

Dear Sir,

Subject – Order for Water Pumps.

Thank you very much for your letter dated 30 April 2003 offering quotation for the water pumps of our requirement.
We are pleased to inform you that your quotation has been found most reasonable.
I hereby place the order for these pumps as describe below-

| SN | Item | Description | Quantity being ordered |
|---|---|---|---|
| 1 | Varuna | Half Horse Power, inlet = half inch, outlet = half inch, | 100 units |
|  | Water pump | 1500,RPM and self priming | Hundred units |

We are sending a DD of Rs 300000=00 (three lakh only) with this letter as full payment of the water pumps. We are sure that you shall receive this order well before 15 May 2003.

We hope that the delivery of the pumps will be complete well before 30 June. 2003.

Please send the pumps properly packed in damage proof cartoons by an insured rail transport only.

Thank you very much for your catalog containing the latest range of water pumps. At present, we need the above-mentioned pump only. However, if we need any one from your latest range of pumps, we will certainly place the order in this regard.

Thanks,

Regards,


Mahesh Varma
The Purchase Manager

RCM-VS

***

# <u>Letter of Claim or Complaint</u>
## <u>Some more letters</u>
## <u>Complaint about short supply/wrong supply and corrupt hard disc</u>


**Subject Matter for the letter**

Assume that you are the Purchase Manager in Laxmi Sponge and Steel Ltd Maihar Road Satna (MP).. You placed an order for fifty desktop computers, with Dolphin Computers Ltd. Lawrence Towers 25 Inner Ring Road Greater Noida (UP), all with TFT monitors and supported by UPS Systems. But you have received a short supply of three UPS Systems and two desktop computers with ordinary color monitors. Besides this, during installation, it was found that two computers were taking too long to boot and your computer experts declared that they had corrupt hard discs. Write a letter of complaint.

**Answer:**

# Laxmi Sponge and Steel Ltd.

**Maihar Road Satna (MP) 485001**
**Phones-0762-3035449, 50, 51,52,53,**
**E-mail – laxmispongesteel@rediffmail.com**
**Visit us on laxmispongesteel.com**

15 April, 2003

Your Reference-S-Q-DC-12459
Our Reference – P – Cl - 467567

**The Sales Manager**
**Dolphin Computers Ltd.**
**Lawrence Towers**
**25 Inner Ring Road**
**Greater Noida (UP), 110016**

Dear Sir,

Subject – Complaint about short / wrong supply and computer with corrupt hard disc

I regret to bring it to your kind consideration that we have received a short supply of three UPS Systems in the lot of 50 computers sent by you to us as per our order (Invoice No. DC – 1278 dated 10 April 2003). The same lot has a wrong supply of two ordinary color monitors. Besides this, two computers of this very lot have corrupt hard discs.

On 12 April, 2003, when our store manager received the consignment and opened it for inspection, he found it short by three UPS Systems. We had ordered for 50 UPS Systems but we received only 47 UPS Systems.
While on the other hand, further inspection revealed that two color monitors were of wrong specifications. We had ordered for 50 TFT monitors but we received 48 TFT monitors and two ordinary color monitors.
Another problem that came to light during installation was that two computers were taking too long to boot. Our computer experts say that they have corrupt hard discs and must be replaced with new ones.

I am proud to say that we never received any complaints with your product, service and supply. It is for the first time that we have encountered such a problem with your product

However, I am sure that you will provide a suitable solution to this problem very soon i.e. sending two UPS Systems of our requirements, taking back two ordinary color monitors, providing us with two TFT monitors in place of them, and replacing the corrupt hard discs of our two computers with new hard discs.
Thanks,

Truly yours,


Prashant Mishra
The Purchase Manager

Encl. 1. A certificate of short and wrong supply
        from our Store Manager
      2. A certificate of malfunction
        from our Computer Expert

RBP-MB

***

# Letter of Adjustment
## Reply to the above letter

# Dolphin Computers Ltd.
**Lawrence Towers 25 Inner Ring Road**
**Greater Noida (UP), 110016**
**Phones-011-23035439, 40, 41,42,43,Fax-011-23035460, 61, 62,63,4**
**E-mail –dolphincomputers@rediffmail.com**
**Visit us on dolphincomputers.com**

15 April, 2003

Your Reference- P – Cl - 467567
Our Reference – S- Adj - 356786

**The Purchase  Manager**
**Laxmi Sponge and Steel Ltd.**
**Maihar Road Satna (MP) 485001**

Dear Sir,

Subject – Adjustment against short / wrong supply and computers with corrupt hard discs

I am awfully sorry to note that you have received a short supply of three UPS Systems and a wrong supply of two ordinary color monitors. Besides this, another complaint is that two computers of this lot have corrupt hard discs.

I am sorry for the inconvenience caused due to this fault on our side. However, I assure you that everything will be alright very soon and you need not worry about anything. I thank you for informing us in time. I am grateful to you for this.

Now, I request you to contact our local agent on the contact number / address given below:-

Sarala Infotech Pvt. Ltd.
12 Adarsh Nagar Satna (MP)
Phones – 07672- 254676, 234687 or M- 9987356432

We have already instructed them in this regard. They have ready stock and expert hands to deal with this problem. They will replace the corrupt hard discs of your computers besides supplying you three UPS Systems which are short and two TFT monitors of your requirements. Please return them the two ordinary color monitors which you have not ordered.

I once again regret the inconvenience caused to you but I hope that we are alert enough now and no such incident will take place again in future.
Thank you very much,

With great regards,


Rajesh Singh
The Sales Manager

RCP-LM

***

# <u>One More Letter of Complaint</u>

**Q.** Assume that you are Ravi Sharma the Purchase Manager in Swastika Cement Ltd Maihar Road Katni. You placed an order for 20 air conditioners for your offices with Chillblast Cooling Systems Pvt. Ltd. Satyam Towers VS Road Greater Noida (UP). After the installation of air conditioners, you found that some of them are not working properly. They stop cooling intermittently. They are within the guarantee period. Write a letter of complaint.

Ans.

# Swastika Cement Ltd.
### Maihar Road Katni (MP) 486002
### Phones-07674-3035449, 50, 51,52,53,
### E-mail – swastikacement@rediffmail.com
### Visit us on swastikacement.com

21 May, 2003

Reference – P – Cl – 497

**The Sales Manager**
**Chillblast Cooling Systems Pvt. Ltd.**
**Satyam Towers VS Road**
**Greater Noida (UP) 120098**

Dear Sir,

Subject – Complaint about malfunctioning air conditioners:

I regret to inform you that the air conditioners sent by you (Invoice Number- AC – 93532 Dated – 5 May 2003) as per our order dated 25 April 2003 (Ref-P-Ord-26647), are not functioning properly, after working nicely for a week.

Out of twenty air conditioners of this lot, eighteen are working very nicely but two of them are mal-functional. They stop cooling intermittently. These air conditioners bear a two-year warranty offered by you as per the quotation sent by you (Ref.-S-Q-F-14334, Dated 15 April 2003).

I request you to take necessary action in this regard i.e. get them repaired very soon as per the warranty offered by you.
I am sure that our grievances shall be listened to and provided for.
Thanks,

Faithfully yours,


Ravi Sharma
The Purchase Manager

Encl. A copy of certificate
        issued by our Maintenance Engineer.

RCS-PNV

***

# <u>Adjustment Letter</u>
### <u>Reply to the above letter</u>

# Chillblast Cooling Systems Pvt. Ltd.
**Satyam Towers VS Road Greater Noida (UP) 120098**
**Phones-012-2035439, 40, 41, 42, 43,**
**Email – chillblastsystems@rediffmail.com**
**Visit us on chillblastcoolingsystems.com**

25 May, 2003

Your Reference-P-Cl-497
Our Reference-S-Adj-13

**The Purchase Manager**
**Swastika Cement Ltd.**
**Maihar Road Katni (MP) 486002**

Dear Sir,

Subject – Your complaint about non-functional air conditioners:

I am very much sorry to note that two out of twenty air conditioners supplied to you by us as per your order dated 25 April 2003 (Ref-P-Ord-26647), are not functioning properly.
We have noted your complaint and we will get them fixed very soon. You need not worry about them at all.
I request you to contact our local agent at the following contact information. :-
Savera Enterprises
15 Nehru Nagar Katni (MP)
585067
Phones- 07677-430876- M- 9887654034
We have sent them instructions in this regard. They have expert engineers to repair the malfunction of your air conditioners. They will visit you very soon.
I thank you very much for your cooperation and for informing us in time. Please feel free to inform us of the further troubles if you encounter any in our further dealings.
I promise you that no such incident shall ever take place in future again.

Thank you very much,

Kind regards,

Mohan Karat
The Sales Manager

RKD-SM

***

# <u>Sales Letter</u>

A sales letter is a letter that is written to a prospective buyer with a view to persuading him to buy a product. This letter is generally written to old customers and prospective buyers selected through a process when a new product is launched or old product is modified with special features.

Most important feature of this letter is that it bears some necessary sales punches which successfully attract the customer, e.g. discounts and gifts.

## <u>Sample Sales Letter</u>

# Exon Pumps Pvt. Ltd.

## 35 SR Complex Industrial Area Adyar
## Chennai Tamil Nadu -  440099

**Phones-044-23435429, 30,31,32,33,**
**E-mail – exonpumps@rediffmail.com**
**Visit us on exonpumps.com**

15 April, 2003

Reference- SL - 59

## The Purchase Manager

**Kay Pee Constructions Pvt. Ltd.**
**Sarita Complex ,Third Storey, near Sarai Kale Khan**
**Faridabad (UP) NCR 110029**

Dear Sir,

Subject – Sales Letter

We are an ISO certified water pump manufacturing company, having our strong presence in India since 1949. We manufacture water pumps, submersible pumps for domestic, agricultural and industrial uses. Our pumps are energy efficient, durable, and safe and supported by a three-year warranty.

We have recently manufactured a range of self-priming pumps ranging from ½ to 100 horsepower pumps including submersible pumps for housing colonies or various other purposes.
At present we are giving 20% discount on all pumps and a 10% cash purchase discount on the purchase of more than one lakh.

Please go through the catalog enclosed for detailed information about our product.

I am sure that you will find our products very suitable to your housing colonies and other projects.
If you have any suggestions regarding our products / services, please let us know.

Thanks,

Yours faithfully,


Mahesh Varma
The Sales Manager

Encl- Catalog

RCM-VS

***

# Credit Letter

'Purchase on credit' and 'pay after sales' has become very popular in the world of work. Since the traders and retailers have to maintain a lot of variety to attract the customers, much of their business depends upon the credit.

Although selling on credit may be a risky affair, leading to nonpayment, a dispute, or unnecessary wastage of time and money, a substantial amount of sale is based on credit itself.

A letter making a request for credit is known as 'Credit Letter'. The following precautions should be kept in mind while writing this letter:-

1. State why you are not able to go in for cash purchase.
2. State your selling potentials as well as those of the product or goods.
3. State clearly the desired period and terms of credit.
4. Provide credit references eg the name, address and phone numbers of the banks with whom you do business besides providing the name, address and phone numbers of the manufacturers / financers with whom you have credit terms.
5. Promise to provide all the related information if asked for.

**Subject Matter for the letter**

Assume that you are Vikram Gupta the Purchase Manager in Kalpana Traders 353 B Mathura Complex AB Road Agra (UP), dealing with the whole sale of tyres and tubes. You have come to know about a new brand (Plaza Tyres) whose popularity is on the increase. Write a letter to Plaza Tyres Ltd. Vakola Santacruz East Mumbai, requesting for a credit purchase of 200 tyres for two months.

## Sample Credit Letter

# Kalpana Traders Ltd.

**353/B Mathura Complex AB Road**
**Agra (UP) - 120011**
**Phones-012-23435429, 30,31,32,33,Fax-044-23435460, 61, 62,63,4**
**Email –kalpanatraders@rediffmail.com**
**Visit us on kalpanatraders.com**

15 April, 2003

Reference- Cre –PT-001

**The Sales Manager**
**Plaza Tyres Pvt. Ltd.**
**Vakola SantaCruz East**
**Mumbai  220029**

Dear Sir,

Subject – Request for Credit Purchase

We are wholesale dealers of tyres and tubes for the west UP and sell almost all the popular and important brands of Indian and foreign make. Our annual turnover ranges between 2 to 3 crores.

We have come to know about the popularity and quality of Plaza Tyres through a business associate of ours in Mumbai

We want to include Plaza Tyres too in our showroom..

Our survey indicates that there is a big market for Plaza Tyres in Agra and surrounding areas.

But it is very difficult to maintain cash purchases of all the items in our showroom.

Therefore, I request you to supply 200 tyres on credit for two months as mentioned below:-

| SN | Item Description | Quantity in numbers |
|---|---|---|
| 1 | Plaza Radial Car Tyre | 100 |
| 2 | Plaza Elephant Tractor Tyre | 50 |
| 3 | Plaza Steel grip Motor Cycle Tyre | 25 |
| 4 | Plaza Steel grip Scooter Tyre | 25 |
| 5 | Total | 200 Tyres |

We will pay the whole amount by the end of the second month from the date we receive the delivery.

Our Bankers are:-

(i) State bank of India

    AB Road Agra (UP) Phone 235876

(i) Punjab National Bank

    Agra Cantt Agra (UP)

We have our credit accounts with the following tyre manufacturing companies:-

(i) Apollo Tyres Ltd.

    Shree Vihar BK Chatterjee Road

    Kolkata 450463

    Phones – 013 – 50304090, 91, 92

(ii) TVS Tyres Ltd

    Shyama Complex International Dwarka

    New Delhi 110013

    Phones – 011 – 2375643, 64

You can make inquiries for your satisfaction and if you need any further information, please do write to us.

I am sure that you will consider our request with a view to increasing the sale of your products.

Thanks,


Yours faithfully,



Mahesh Varma
The Purchase Manager

*****

# <u>Accepting the request for credit purchase</u>

You already know about the 'pay after sale' phenomena which is very popular in the world of trade. Thus if it is found that the firm requesting for credit purchase has potentials to pay within the promised time frame, its  request for credit purchase may be granted.

Observe the following precautions, if you are writing the letter granting request for credit purchase:-

1. Disclose in the very beginning that their request has been granted.
2. Explain your terms of credit clearly.
3. State clearly which benefits you offer or do not offer to credit purchasers.
4. Mention the credit references on the basis of which you have granted the credit purchase.

**Subject Matter for the letter**

Assume that you are A.S. Nigam, the sales Manager in Plaza Tyres Ltd. Vakola Santacruz East Mumbai, you receive a letter from Kalpana Traders 353 B Mathura Complex AB Road Agra (UP), asking for credit purchase. After verifying the credit references you find the party honest and having potential to pay back. Write a letter granting their request for credit purchase of 200 tyres for two months.

# Plaza Tyres Pvt. Ltd.

## Vakola Santacruz East
## Mumbai - 220011

**Phones-022-23435429, 30,31,32,33**
**E-mail – plazatyres@rediffmail.com**
**Visit us on plazatyres.com**

19 April, 2003

Your Reference- Cre –PT-001
Our  Reference – C- 0001


**The Purchase Manager**
Kalpana Traders Ltd.
353/B Mathura Complex AB Road
Agra (UP) -  120011

Dear Sir,

Subject – Supply of Plaza Tyres on credit

We are pleased to inform you that your request for credit purchase has been granted. Your order for 200 Plaza Tyres as per your request and as mentioned in the following table is being sent immediately by Super Cargo Ltd Mumbai.

| SN | Item Description | Quantity in numbers | Price per unit | Total |
|---|---|---|---|---|
| 1 | Plaza Radial Car Tyre | 100 | Rs 8000 | Rs 800000 |
| 2 | Plaza Elephant Tractor Tyre | 50 | Rs 12000 | Rs 600000 |
| 3 | Plaza Steel grip Motor Cycle Tyre | 25 | Rs 1200 | Rs 30000 |
| 4 | Plaza Steel grip Scooter Tyre | 25 | Rs 800 | Rs18000 |
| 5 | Grand Total | 200 Tyres | NA | Rs 1448000 |

A bill of Rs 1303200 (Rs thirteen lakh thirty two hundred only) is being enclosed with this letter.

You will see that although you  are our credit  customer yet we have given the usual discount of  10%

The last date of the payment is 15 April 2003. To avail the discount benefit, your payment of the credit must be made before 15 April 2003. The DD that you send us, must reach us by 15 April 2003

The company believes in cash sales and we do not have any credit customers. But looking at your sales potentials, and your goodwill the policy has been relaxed.

To maintain our credit record, we are sending a form with this letter. Please fill it and send us a copy of it as soon as you get the delivery of the consignment.

Thanks,

Yours faithfully,

The Sales Manager

Encl.1.A copy of bill
    2.  Credit Information Form

RCM-VS

***

# <u>Refusing the request for credit purchase</u>

Although, 'pay after sales' is very popular yet it may not always be trustworthy. It is a risky affair and may lead to loss of money and time besides leading to a legal dispute. That is why companies generally follow safe passage and refuse credit purchase.

Thus it is quite possible that you may have to refuse such a credit purchase. Or you may have to refuse credit purchase on finding that payment / sales potentials or good will of the firm is not satisfactory.

In this case keep the following points in your mind:-

1.  Offer thanks for the request and the interest shown in buying our product.
2.  Say 'no' but politely.
3.  Do mention the reason why it is not possible.

4. Do indicate the possibility of credit purchase in future if the policy changes.
5. Encourage the party to make cash purchases by offering a discount for cash payment.
6. Advise the party to buy less quantity instead of a bulk quantity.

**Subject Matter for the letter**

Assume that you are A.S. Nigam, the sales Manager in  Plaza Tyres Ltd. Vakola Santacruz East Mumbai, You receive a letter from  Kalpana Traders 353 B Mathura Complex AB Road Agra (UP),asking for credit purchase. Write a letter of refusal.

# Plaza Tyres Pvt. Ltd.
## Vakola Santacruz East
## Mumbai -  220011
**Phones-022-23435429, 30,31,32,33**
**E-mail – plazatyres@rediffmail.com**
**Visit us on plazatyres.com**

19 April, 2003

Your Reference- Cre –PT-001
Our  Reference – C-R- 0001

**The Purchase Manager**
Kalpana Traders Ltd.
353/B Mathura Complex AB Road
Agra (UP) -  120011

Dear Sir,

Subject – Refusal to credit

Thank you very much for your letter requesting credit and the interest shown in buying our products.

We have examined your credit potentials through your bankers and the companies where you have your credit accounts, but they do not meet our requirements

Therefore at present it is not possible for us to provide the facility of credit purchase.

However if the policy is relaxed at a later time, we would certainly inform you.

We would like to advise you to purchase a smaller number of tyres so that you are able to pay cash for them. We are offering a 15% discount on all cash purchases.

In this way you will be able to keep contact with us and if the policy changes, you will be able to avail the benefits the company offers to its customers from time to time.

Thanks,

Yours faithfully,


Mahesh Varma
The Sales Manager

RCM-VS

***

# <u>Collection Letter</u>

You already know about 'Purchase on credit' and 'pay after sales' and how you can request for credit besides knowing how to accept credit terms or refuse to sell on credit. However, if you have accepted to sell on credit, you shall have to collect your money from your creditors. Thus the letter written with a view to collect the money from the creditors is known as the collection letter. Generally, you will find that your creditors are paying you money as they have agreed but some of them may be late or stop making any response. Such creditors may be in real difficulty also and you must know that this is a sensitive issue too and you need to act tactfully to get your money back. At the initial stage, collection letters are written to remind them that they were not able to pay the money as they promised. You may have to send a couple of reminders before you get your money back. In tough cases, you may have to write a series of such letters (reminder after reminder) and finally serve a notice to the creditors for legal action against him.

If you are going to write this letter, keep the following points in your mind:-

1. Like the letter of complaint or adjustment, this letter too requires tactful handling. Thus, we need to be calm, courteous, and patient. Losing temper will aggravate the matter.
2. We have to collect the money tactfully by arousing in the mind of the debtor, a sense of justice, honesty, fairness and fear of good will loss and termination of further benefits, facilities and contact.
3. We must give some appropriate time gap between the two reminders.
4. When the reminders don't work the last letter is given as notice for legal action.

**Subject Matter for the letter**

Assume that you are A.S. Nigam, the sales Manager in  Plaza Tyres Ltd. Vakola Santacruz East Mumbai, Youhave sold tyres to Kalpana Traders 353 B Mathura Complex AB Road Agra (UP) as per their request. But after paying a major portion of the amount, they have stopped paying any further. Write a letter of reminder

.

## Sample Collection Letter

# Plaza Tyres Pvt. Ltd.

**Vakola Santacruz East**
**Mumbai -  220011**
Phones-022-23435429, 30,31,32,33
E-mail – plazatyres@rediffmail.com
Visit us on plazatyres.com

19 Sep, 2004


Your Reference- Cre –PT-001
Our  Reference – C- Rem - 01


**The Purchase Manager**
Kalpana Traders Ltd.
353/B Mathura Complex AB Road
Agra (UP) -  120011


Dear Sir,


Subject – Payment of credit


I am writing this letter to remind you of the balance payment of Rs 3 lakhs for the credit purchase of Plaza Tyres.
You made an overall credit of Rs 1448000 out of which you have paid Rs 1148000 in three installments but Rs 300000 is still pending unpaid with us.

I am sure that you must have sold all the tyres. We already offered a 10% discount but you could not avail it because you could not pay the full amount by the due date.

However, we have accepted the payment in installments and only a fraction of it is unpaid but we have not received any money for six months.

You can pay this amount also in small installments. We are ready to have credit relations with you although it is very difficult to maintain credit relations nowadays.

I am sure that you will respect your goodwill and standing in the market and pay the balance amount in full or in installments.

We shall be very happy to extend any support you need from us.

Thanks,

Yours faithfully,


Mahesh Varma
The Sales Manager

Encl.1.A copy of bill
    2.  Credit Information

RCM-VS

***

## <u>Second Reminder</u>

If the reminder sent by you doesn't work, after a proper interval of time ( at least a month) you can send another reminder as shown below:-


## <u>Second Reminder</u>

# Plaza Tyres Pvt. Ltd.

**Vakola Santacruz East**
**Mumbai -  220011**
**Phones-022-23435429, 30,31,32,33**
**E-mail – plazatyres@rediffmail.com**
**Visit us on plazatyres.com**

19 Oct, 2004

Your Reference- Cre –PT-001
Our  Reference – C- Rem – 02

**The Purchase Manager**
Kalpana Traders Ltd.
353/B Mathura Complex AB Road
Agra (UP) -  120011

Dear Sir,

Subject – Second Reminder to the Payment of credit

Please refer to our reminder dated 19 Sep 2004 sent to you by us for the balance payment of Rs 300000 towards the credit purchase of Plaza Tyres.
This is our second attempt to remind you of the balance payment.
We don't want to spoil our relations with you. You must realize that it is too late.
Please realize the payment as soon as possible.

Thanks,

Yours faithfully,

Mahesh Varma
The Sales Manager

Encl.1.A copy of bill
    2.  Credit Information

RCM-VS

***

# <u>Third Reminder</u>

# **Plaza Tyres Pvt. Ltd.**
**Vakola Santacruz East**
**Mumbai -  220011**
**Phones-022-23435429, 30,31,32,33**
**E-mail – plazatyres@rediffmail.com**
**Visit us on plazatyres.com**

19 Nov, 2004
Your Reference- Cre –PT-001
Our  Reference – C- Rem – 03

The  Purchase  Manager
Kalpana Traders  Ltd.
353/B Mathura Complex AB Road
Agra (UP) -  120011

Dear Sir,

Subject – Third Reminder to the Payment of credit

This is our third attempt in connection to the balance payment
of Rs 300000 that you owe to us towards the credit purchase of
Plaza Tyres.

If by chance you could not get our earlier letters, you must get this letter because we are sending this letter by a registered post.
We don't want to damage your goodwill and reputation. We want to avoid a legal dispute with you. We still believe that you will honor the terms and conditions already agreed by us. Please do expedite the payment the payment by 31 Oct 2004

Thanks,

Yours faithfully,


Mahesh Varma
The Sales Manager

Encl.1.A copy of bill
   2.  Credit Information

RCM-VS

## <u>Fourth and Final Reminder</u>

# Plaza Tyres Pvt. Ltd.
## Vakola Santacruz East
## Mumbai -  220011
Phones-022-23435429, 30,31,32,33
E-mail – plazatyres@rediffmail.com
Visit us on plazatyres.com

19 Dec, 2004
Your Reference- Cre –PT-001

Our  Reference – C- Rem - 01

The  Purchase  Manager
Kalpana Traders  Ltd.
353/B Mathura Complex AB Road
Agra (UP) -  120011

Dear Sir,

Subject – Fourth and final Reminder to the Payment of credit

This is our fourth and final attempt in connection to the balance payment of Rs 300000 that you owe to us towards the credit purchase of Plaza Tyres.
Unless we receive a DD of Rs 300000 (three lakh) as the balance payment of tyres purchased by you from us on credit by 15 Non 2004, we will place the matter in the hands of our legal advisor for further action.


Thanks,

Yours faithfully,


Mahesh Varma
The Sales Manager

Encl.1.A copy of bill
    2.  Credit Information

RCM-VS

$$*\!*\!*$$

**Useful and Important Sentences on General Business
Correspondence**

1.  I hope this letter has good business for you.

2.  I am writing to inquire about your services.

3.  Please find attached the documents you requested.

4.  I am writing to inform you of a recent development.

5.  We appreciate your prompt response to our previous correspondence.

6.  We would like to schedule a meeting to discuss this further.

7.  Thank you for your time and consideration.

8.  We are pleased to inform you that your application has been approved.

9.  Please confirm receipt of this letter.

10.     We look forward to your response.

11. Kindly review the attached proposal and provide your feedback.

12.     We are writing to request a quotation for the following services.

13.     We apologize for any inconvenience this may have caused.

14.     We are writing to follow up on our previous communication.

15.     We would like to express our appreciation for your continued support.

16.	We are interested in learning more about your product offerings.

17.	Please let us know if you require any additional information.

18.	We regret to inform you that your request has been denied.

19.	Your cooperation in this matter is highly appreciated.

20.	We are writing to confirm our appointment scheduled for (date).

21.	Please provide us with a detailed report on this matter.

22.	We are excited to announce our new product launch.

23.	We would like to propose a partnership between our companies.

24.	We are pleased to invite you to our upcoming event.

25.	Your feedback is valuable to us.

26.	We are writing to request an update on the current status.

27.	Thank you for bringing this matter to our attention.

28.	We would appreciate your immediate attention to this issue.

29.	We are confident that this collaboration will be mutually beneficial.

30.	Please find the enclosed check for payment.

31.	We are writing to request a meeting at your earliest convenience.

32.	We would like to discuss the terms of our agreement.

33.	We are grateful for your prompt action on this matter.

34.	We are writing to request a formal extension of the deadline.

35.	We would like to express our interest in your latest product.

36.	We are writing to provide you with an update on the project.

37.	Please find the attached invoice for your records.

38.	We are writing to request a refund for the defective product.

39.	We would like to thank you for your recent order.

40.	We are writing to notify you of a change in our contact details.

41.	We would appreciate it if you could expedite this process.

42.	We are writing to request your assistance with this matter.

43.	We are writing to confirm our order for the following items.

44.	We would like to express our satisfaction with your services.

45.	We are writing to address a concern regarding your recent delivery.

46.	We would like to schedule a conference call to discuss this issue.

47.      Please let us know your availability for a meeting.

48.      We are writing to request a copy of the contract.

49.      We would like to express our regret for any inconvenience caused.

50.      We are pleased to confirm the details of our agreement.

## Sales and Marketing

1.  We are excited to introduce our new line of products.

2.  We believe our products will meet your needs.

3.  Please find enclosed our latest catalog.

4.  We are offering a special discount for early orders.

5.  We would like to offer you a complimentary sample.

6.  We are confident that you will find our products satisfactory.

7.  We look forward to your order.

8.  Please let us know if you have any questions about our products.

9.  We are writing to follow up on your inquiry.

10.      We are pleased to offer you a 10% discount on your next purchase.

11. We hope you will take advantage of our current promotion.

12.      Please find enclosed our latest promotional brochure.

13.      We are writing to introduce our new sales representative.

14.	We believe you will be interested in our latest offering.

15.	We would like to schedule a product demonstration.

16.	We are writing to thank you for your recent purchase.

17.	We are confident that our products will exceed your expectations.

18.	Please let us know how we can assist you with your order.

19.	We are offering a limited-time discount on our services.

20.	We hope you will consider our proposal.

**Customer Service**

1.  We are writing to acknowledge your complaint.

2.  We apologize for any inconvenience this may have caused.

3.  We are committed to resolving this issue promptly.

4.  Please provide us with additional details regarding your complaint.

5.  We appreciate your patience and understanding.

6.  We are writing to confirm receipt of your return.

7.  We will process your refund within the next 7 business days.

8.  We are sorry to hear about your negative experience.

9.  We value your feedback and will use it to improve our services.

10.	We are writing to inform you that your request has been approved.

11. We are currently investigating the issue and will update you soon.

12.       We appreciate your business and look forward to serving you again.

13.       We are writing to offer a solution to the problem you reported.

14.       Please let us know if you need any further assistance.

15.       We are dedicated to providing excellent customer service.

## Finance and Accounting

1.  Please find enclosed the invoice for your recent purchase.

2.  We are writing to remind you of the upcoming payment deadline.

3.  We have received your payment and thank you for your promptness.

4.  Please contact us if you have any questions regarding this invoice.

5.  We are writing to request a financial statement for the last quarter.

6.  We are pleased to confirm receipt of your payment.

7.  We are writing to notify you of an outstanding balance on your account.

8.  We appreciate your timely attention to this matter.

9.  Please find the attached financial report for your review.

10.       We are writing to request an extension on our credit terms.

11. We are writing to clarify a discrepancy in your account.

12.        Please let us know if there are any issues with this payment.

13.        We are grateful for your prompt settlement of the account.

14.        We would like to discuss a payment plan for the outstanding balance.

15.        Please confirm receipt of this payment and update our records accordingly.

## Thank You Notes

1. Thank you so much for your generous gift.

2. I appreciate your kindness and thoughtfulness.

3. Thank you for your hospitality during my visit.

4. I am grateful for your support and friendship.

5. Thank you for the lovely flowers you sent.

6. Your generosity means the world to me.

7. Thank you for being there when I needed you most.

8. I truly appreciate your help and assistance.

9. Thank you for the wonderful dinner party.

10.        Your thoughtfulness is greatly appreciated.

## Apologies

1. I apologize for any inconvenience I may have caused.

2. I am truly sorry for my actions.

3. Please accept my sincerest apologies.

4. I regret any hurt my words may have caused.

5. I am sorry and I will ensure it doesn't happen again.

6.  I hope you can forgive me for my mistake.

7.  I apologize for the misunderstanding.

8.  I am sorry for any trouble I may have caused.

9.  Please accept my apology and know that I value our relationship.

10.     I am deeply sorry for any distress I may have caused you.

## Opening Statements

1.  I hope this email finds you well.

2.  I am writing to you regarding (subject).

3.  I am writing to follow up on our previous conversation.

4.  I hope you are having a productive week.

5.  I wanted to reach out to discuss (topic).

6.  I am writing to inform you about (update).

7.  I hope you are doing well.

8.  I wanted to touch base with you about (subject).

9.  I am writing to request (information/action).

10.     I hope you had a great weekend.

## Requests and Inquiries

1.  Could you please provide me with (specific information)?

2.  I would appreciate it if you could send me (document/report).

3.  Can you confirm the details of our meeting?

4.  Please let me know if you need any further information.

5.  I am seeking your approval for (proposal).

6.  Could you clarify (specific point) for me?

7.  I would like to request a meeting to discuss (topic).

8.  Please let me know your availability for a call.

9.  I am interested in learning more about (subject).

10.     Can you please update me on the status of (project)?

**Responses and Follow-Ups**

1.  Thank you for your prompt response.

2.  I appreciate your quick reply.

3.  I wanted to follow up on my previous email.

4.  I am writing to confirm the details of our conversation.

5.  Thank you for providing the requested information.

6.  I am still waiting for your response regarding (subject).

7.  Please find attached the requested document.

8.  I have received your email and will get back to you shortly.

9.  Thank you for bringing this to my attention.

10.     I will review the information and get back to you.

**Announcements and Updates**

1.  I am pleased to inform you that (update).

2.  We are excited to announce (event/change).

3.  I wanted to share some important news with you.

4.  Please be advised that (update).

5.  We are writing to notify you of (change).

6.  I am writing to update you on (project/status).

7.  We are pleased to announce (new product/service).

8.  Please note that (important change) will take effect on (date).

9.  I wanted to let you know about (event/issue).

10.  We are delighted to inform you that (achievement).

**Closing Statements**

1.  Thank you for your attention to this matter.

2.  Please feel free to contact me if you have any questions.

3.  I look forward to your response.

4.  Thank you for your cooperation.

5.  Please let me know if you need any further assistance.

6.  I appreciate your help with this matter.

7.  Looking forward to working with you.

8.  I am looking forward to our meeting.

9.  Thank you for your understanding.

10.  Best regards, (Your Name).

# Part 8

# *Banking Correspondence*

*This
Part
Contains
The
Letters
That
Are
Written
To
Banks*

# Banking Correspondence

Correspondence with banks is an essential part of business correspondence. Banks provide several important services e.g. savings bank account, current account, automated teller machine, debit cards, credit cards, loan, and overdraft etc. Banks too are business houses whether private or public. They too are facing stiff competition. Thus frequent correspondence with banks on several affairs is quite natural. Some important letters to banks are given here:-

## Letter to Bank Requesting Overdraft Facility

# Plaza Tyres Pvt. Ltd.
### Shamshabad Road Agra -  282001
**Phones-022-23435429, 30,31,32,33,Fax-022-23435460,**
**E-mail –plazatyres@rediffmail.com**

19 April, 2003
Reference- B-OD –001

**The Branch Manager**
**State Bank of India Main Branch**
**353/B Mathura Complex AB Road**
**Agra (UP) - 120011**

Dear Sir,

Subject – Requirement of Overdraft Facility

We have Our Current Account No. 8268878654 with your bank and we have been having banking transactions with you for the last ten years.

We have always maintained a large balance of at least Rs. 20,00,00 = 00 ( Rs. Two lakh) in our account at any point of time. We appreciate the kind of service you are providing us.

We are at present expanding our business substantially so we will need more money for our present needs and investment from time to time. In this regard, we seek an overdraft facility of Rs. 10, 00, 000 = 00 from you.

We enclose copies of Balance Sheets for the last three financial years. Besides this, we also enclose the papers of our property on the basis of which we want the overdraft facility. The undersigned will be pleased to call on you and explain our stand.

Thanks,

Yours faithfully,


Mahesh Varma


The Sales Manager

Enclosure: 1. Balance Sheet
          2. Papers of property

RCM-VD


***


# Letter to Bank Requesting Increase in Overdraft Value

# Plaza Tyres Pvt. Ltd.

**ShamshabadRoad Agra -  110023**

**Phones-022-23435429, 30,31,32,33,Fax-022-23435460,**

**E-mail –plazatyres@rediffmail.com**

19 April, 2003
Reference- B-OD – 011

**The Branch Manager**
**State Bank of India Main Branch**
**353/B Mathura Complex AB Road**
**Agra (UP) - 120011**

Dear Sir,

Subject – Increase in the Overdraft Value

We have Our Current Account No. 8268878654 with your bank and we have been doing business with you for the last ten years.

We have always maintained a large balance of at least Rs. 20,00,00 = 00 ( Rs. Two lakh) in our account at any point of time. We appreciate the kind of service you are providing us.
We are getting an overdraft facility of Rs 10,00,000=00 from you and we thank you for extending this facility to us because it has been very helpful to us in extending our business.
However, we request you to increase the overdraft value from Rs 10,00,000=00 to Rs 15,00,000=00 because we at present have to invest an even greater amount of money which we are quite hopeful that it will generate a much greater amount of money. We have always paid our dues on time and we are your old customer.

We enclose copies of Balance Sheets for the last three financial years. Please see the value of the property that we have attached to get the overdraft facility.

The undersigned will be pleased to call on you and explain our stand.

Thanks,

Yours faithfully,

Mahesh Varma


The Sales Manager

Enclosure: 1. Balance Sheet
           2. Papers of property
RCM-VD

***

# <u>Letter to Bank to open a Current Account</u>

# Plaza Tyres Pvt. Ltd.

**Shamshabad Road Agra -  110023**
**Phones-022-23435429, 30,31,32,33,Fax-022-23435460,**
**E-mail –plazatyres@rediffmail.com**

19 April, 2003
Reference- B-OA – 011

**The Branch Manager**
**State Bank of India Main Branch**
**353/B Mathura Complex AB Road**
**Agra (UP) - 120011**

Dear Sir,

Subject – Opening a current account

I would like to open a Current Account in your bank. In this regard, I am enclosing an introduction letter given by Mr. A.P. Tripathi, High-tech Electronics situated at 3, Taj Road, Agra, who is holding a current account with you. His account number is SRG 43262.

Should you require any specific details, please indicate. It will be my pleasure to furnish the same.

I look forward to having banking operations with you for a long time to come.

Thanking you,

Yours faithfully,


Mahesh Varma

The Sales Manager

Enclosure: Introduction Letter

RCM-VD

***

# <u>Letter to Bank to open Savings Bank Account</u>

# Plaza Tyres Pvt. Ltd.
**Shamshabad RoadAgra- 110023**

**Phones-022-23435429, 30,31,32,33, Fax-022-23435460,**
**E-mail –plazatyres@rediffmail.com**

19 April, 2003
Reference- B-OA – 016

**The Branch Manager**
**State Bank of India Main Branch**
**353/B Mathura Complex AB Road**
**Agra (UP) - 120011**

Dear Sir,

Subject: Opening three savings bank accounts

I would like to open three Savings Bank Accounts in your branch in the name of three employees who have recently joined our organization. Since they don't have accounts in the State Bank of India, I am introducing them to you. My account number is 8796546778 — Name- Rajesh Kumar 7 Adarsh Nagar Agra. I am sure that my introduction to these employees is sufficient. However, if you want more people as introducers, I shall be happy to provide the details to you.

Thanking you,


Yours faithfully,


Rajesh Kumar

The Finance Manager
Plaza Tyres Ltd Agra

RCM-VD

***

# Letter to Bank Requesting Statement

# Plaza Tyres Pvt. Ltd.
### Shamshabad Road Agra - 110023
**Phones-022-23435429, 30,31,32,33,Fax-022-23435460,**
**E-mail –plazatyres@rediffmail.com**

3 April, 2019
Reference- B-S – 0114

**The Branch Manager**
**State Bank of India Main Branch**
**353/B Mathura Complex AB Road**
**Agra (UP) -  120011**

Dear Sir,

Subject: Requirement of statement

As you are aware, the current financial year is coming to an end. I would like to request you to provide the statement from 1 January 2019 to 31 March 2019 of our two current accounts:
1. Account No.56987876655 in the name of Plaza Tyres Ltd Agra
and
2. Account No.78609876655 in the name of Savitri Devi Mittal for our perusal at the end of the financial year.


Thanking you,


Yours faithfully,

Rajesh Kumar

The Finance Manager
Plaza Tyres Ltd Agra

RCM-VD


✳✳✳


# <u>Letter to Bank Introducing New Signatory</u>

# Plaza Tyres Pvt. Ltd.
**Shamshabad Road Agra - 110023**
**Phones-022-23435429, 30,31,32,33,Fax-022-23435460,**
**E-mail –plazatyres@rediffmail.com**

1 April, 2019
Reference- B-OTH – 011

**The Branch Manager**
**State Bank of India Main Branch**
**353/B Mathura Complex AB Road**
**Agra (UP) -  120011**

Dear Sir,

Subject: Change in the signatories

Our Senior Finance Manager, Mr. R.K. Kapoor has left our company and he is moving to Bangalore. He was one of the two signatories nominated by our management for signing cheques. In his place, our New Marketing Manager, Mr. T. Dutta is empowered to sign cheques relating to our current account.

Mr. T. Dutta 's signature is shown in the attached slip. For your easy reference he has put his signature thrice.

Henceforth, apart from the undersigned, Mr. T. Dutta will sign all the cheques. We continue to follow our system of having signatures of two executives.

Thanking you,

Yours faithfully,


Rajesh Kumar

The Finance Manager
Plaza Tyres Ltd Agra
Enclosure: Signature Slip

RCM-VD


***

## <u>Letter to Bank Informing Change in the Address</u>

# Plaza Tyres Pvt. Ltd.
### Shamshabad Road Agra -  110023
Phones-022-23435429, 30,31,32,33,Fax-022-23435460,
E-mail –plazatyres@rediffmail.com

6 April, 2019
Reference- B-OTH – 034

**The Branch Manager**
**State Bank of India Main Branch**

353/B Mathura Complex AB Road
Agra (UP) - 120011

Dear Sir,

Subject: Change in the address

On 1 February 2019, we shifted our office and showroom to Fort Road Agra. We have several accounts with your bank. Please change the address of our accounts. I am enclosing the list of our bank accounts along with the name of the account holders with this letter.

Thanking you,

Yours faithfully,


Rajesh Kumar

The Finance Manager
Plaza Tyres Ltd Agra

Encl. A list of account numbers
And name of account holders.

RCM-VD

***

# Letter to Bank Requesting Loan

**Plaza Tyres Pvt. Ltd.**

**ShamshabadRoad Agra - 110023**

**Phones-022-23435429, 30,31,32,33,Fax-022-23435460,**
**E-mail –plazatyres@rediffmail.com**

1 April, 2019
Reference- B-L – 011

**The Branch Manager**
**State Bank of India Main Branch**
**353/B Mathura Complex AB Road**
**Agra (UP) -  120011**

Dear Sir,

Subject: Request for loan

On behalf of Plaza Tyres Pvt. Ltd., I request you to extend us a loan of Rs 50 lakhs in the name of Smt. Veena Devi Mittal, one of the members of our Board of Directors. We have previously taken a loan of Rs. 70 Lakhs from your bank and we have paid the loan in full along with its interest. You can see our previous records, for the eligibility of loan. The account No. of the loan was 8760983478 and it was taken in 2014.
Our sales executive Mr. Ramesh Kaushal will visit your branch to discuss the rates and procedure of the loan.

I look forward to having more transactions and good relations with you.

Thanking you,


Yours faithfully,



Rajesh Kumar

The Finance Manager
Plaza Tyres Ltd Agra

RCM-VD

***

# <u>Letter to Bank Requesting to Dishonour a Cheque</u>

# Plaza Tyres Pvt. Ltd.

**ShamshabadRoad Agra -  110023**
**Phones-022-23435429, 30,31,32,33,Fax-022-23435460,**
**E-mail –plazatyres@rediffmail.com**

1 April, 2019
Reference- B OTH – 012

**The Branch Manager**
**State Bank of India Main Branch**
**353/B Mathura Complex AB Road**
**Agra (UP) - 120011**

Dear Sir,

Subject: Request for dishonouring and blocking the cheques

I am sorry to bring to your notice that our account executive Dashrath Gupta's bag has been stolen from the railway platform Agra. The bag contains a cheque book and a cheque worth three lakh rupees drawn on the name of Smt. Sarita Bharadwaj ( cheque no. 324567). Please don't honour this cheque and block it as well. Besides this, please block the entire series of ten cheques starting from 435621 and ending on 435630. These are the numbers of the cheque book which was in the bag stolen from the railway platform.

Thank you very much for your cooperation.

Yours faithfully,


Rajesh Kumar

The Finance Manager
Plaza Tyres Ltd Agra

RCM-VD

***

## <u>Letter to Bank Asking the Reason behind Dishonouring a Cheque</u>

# Plaza Tyres Pvt. Ltd.
### Shamshabad Road Agra - 110023
Phones-022-23435429, 30,31,32,33, Fax-022-23435460,
E-mail –plazatyres@rediffmail.com

1 April, 2019
Reference- B-OTH – 016

**The Branch Manager**
**State Bank of India Main Branch**
**353/B Mathura Complex AB Road**
**Agra (UP) - 120011**

Dear Sir,

Subject: The cheque dishonoured

I am sorry to bring to your notice that a cheque of Rs. Three lakhs No. 675890 drawn on the name of Rashmi Associates New Delhi dated 23 March 2019 has been dishonoured by your branch.
We always maintain sufficient balance in our accounts and you have extended an overdraft facility of Rs three lakhs as well. Amid these facilities, it is quite disappointing that our cheque has been dishonoured by your branch.
Our accounts executive Ravindra Jain will visit the branch to discuss the matter with you.

Thank you very much for your cooperation.

Yours faithfully,


Rajesh Kumar

The Finance Manager
Plaza Tyres Ltd Agra

RCM-VD


***

# Part 9

# *Insurance Correspondence*

*This
Part
Contains
The
Letters
That
Are
Written
To
Insurance
Companies*

# Insurance Correspondence

Like Banking Correspondence, Insurance Correspondence is also an essential part of business correspondence. Business organizations are in fact risk taking organizations. They invest money on various assets. Therefore, they require insurance on various subjects like risk cover on theft, fire accident, accident, natural calamities, transit loss, medical cover for the employees and their families. Like banks, insurance companies are also business organizations. They may be private and public as well. They are providing risk covers on various subjects and support people and companies to face a sudden calamity, accident or disaster. Thus there is correspondence with insurance companies also. Some important letters to insurance companies are given here:-

## Letter to Insurance Company – Request for Quotation

# Hindustan Computers Ltd

**35 Arera Complex Greater Noida (UP) 110001**
**Phones-012-23435429, 30,31,32,33, Fax-012-234354650, 51, 52,53**
**E-mail – hindustancomputers@rediffmail.com**
**Visit us on hindustancomputers.com**

20 April, 2003
Reference- P – Ins – 23

**The Manager**
**Bharat Insurance Company**
**Bharat Towers Ashoka Road**
**Noida (UP) 110001**

Dear Sir,

Subject: Request for quote

I am writing this letter to request a quote from your company for comprehensive insurance against theft, fire, accident and flood for the head office of my company.

As you see, we assemble and sell computers. We want this policy for our head office. There are fifty one employees including myself, the owner and five security guards. There are fifteen rooms in the building including five offices, a display shop, a large store room and a large workshop for assembling computers.

Please consider the following when calculating the quote:

- The building is safe and we have installed all the fire safety instruments as per the guidance of fire department
- The shop is on high ground, so flood damage, if any, would be minimal
- The shopping center has had no break-in for the past seven years

I would like a quote from your company because my present insurance company just raised my premium, and I believe it is unjustified. I would welcome someone from your company to come to my shop and consider my situation.

Either I or one of my employees will be here Monday – Saturday, from 9am – 6pm, and we would appreciate it if you would call before coming. I can be reached at 9876898765 or at bharatcomputer@gmail.com


Sincerely,


Rakesh Giri
Accounts Manager
Hindustan Computers Ltd.

PS-VKM

***

# <u>Letter to Insurance Company- Request for Transit Insurance</u>

# **Hindustan Computers Ltd**

**35 Arera Complex Greater Noida (UP) 110001**
**Phones-012-23435429, 30,31,32,33, Fax-012-234354650, 51, 52,53**
**E-mail – hindustancomputers@rediffmail.com**
**Visit us on hindustancomputers.com**

21 March, 2004
Reference- P –Ins – 56

**The Manager**
**Bharat Insurance Company**
**Bharat Towers Ashoka Road**
**Noida (UP) 110001**

Dear Sir,

Subject: Request for transit insurance

We have dispatched a consignment of 30 desktop computers from Noida to Gwalior today via Lorry Way, bill No.PR/1062 of Patel Roadways, New Delhi.

The value of desktop computers is Rs.7, 50, 000/-.

We request you to arrange for transport insurance for the amount mentioned above and send your bill for the premium to enable us to send the cheque immediately.

Thanking you,

Yours faithfully,


K.P. Acharya

The Sales manager
Hindustan Computers Noida

RKS-CV

***

## <u>Letter Requesting Group Insurance Cover</u>

# Hindustan Spices Ltd

### 32 Dharmapeth Nagpur 550003
**Phones-043-23435429, 30,31,32,33, Fax-043-234354650, 51, 52,53**
**E-mail – hindustanspices@rediffmail.com**
**Visit us on hindustanspices.com**

2 April, 2005
Reference- P – Ins – 33


**The Manager**
**Bharat Insurance Company**
**Rashmi Vihar Ashoka Road**
**Nagpur 550003**


Dear Sir,

Subject: Group Insurance Cover required

We are pleased to inform you that we are a leading spice
producer located in central India.

In our organization, twenty of our executives are frequent business travelers. We want to take Group Insurance Cover to protect their families in the event of accidents resulting in death during business travel. The sum assured is Rs.3, 00, 000/- for an employee.

Kindly send your application form with a catalog to enable us to proceed further. You may indicate the best policy for us along with the premium charges.

Thanking you,

Yours faithfully,


Ravi Nayak
The Personnel Manager
Hindustan Spices Ltd.

RKV-LV

***

## <u>Letter to Insurance Company Informing about Theft</u>

# Hindustan Computers Ltd

**35 Arera Complex Greater Noida (UP) 110001**
**Phones-012-23435429, 30,31,32,33, Fax-012-234354650, 51, 52,53**
**E-mail – hindustancomputers@rediffmail.com**
**Visit us on hindustancomputers.com**

25 June, 2003
Reference- P – Ins– 788


**The Manager**
**Bharat Insurance Company**
**Bharat Towers Ashoka Road**

Noida (UP) 110001

Dear Sir,

Subject: Information of theft

It is with regret that we have to inform you that a major theft had taken place in our go down at Noida last night. The computer hardware worth Rs. 500000/- has been stolen.
You may kindly note that we have registered a case with the nearby police station in Noida this morning.
We have already taken an insurance policy from your company against theft for a value of Rs.5, 00, 000/- vide our Policy No. ZAC/1016 dated 1st June 1997.

Kindly depute your representative to assess the loss in order that our insurance claim can be settled at the earliest.

Thanking you,

Yours faithfully,
Ravi Kumar Bhargava
The Personnel Manager
Bharat Computers Ltd.

MKP-RKG

***

## <u>Letter to Insurance Company Informing about a Fire Accident</u>

# Hindustan Spices Ltd

**32 Dharampeth Nagpur 550003**
**Phones-043-23435429, 30,31,32,33, Fax-043-234354650, 51, 52,53**
**E-mail – hindustanspices@rediffmail.com**
**Visit us on hindustanspices.com**

23 April, 2006
Reference- P – Ins – 190

**The Manager**
**Bharat Insurance Company**
**Rashmi Vihar Ashoka Road**
**Nagpur 550003**

Dear Sir,

Subject: Information about fire accident

Early this morning, a major fire broke out in our factory premises and gutted finished products, materials and equipment worth Rs.3,50,000. Thanks to the fire brigade's quick action, a possible further loss was arrested.
We have insured our factory against fire accidents for a value of Rs.10,00,000/- vide our Policy No.FA/0026 dated 6th April 1995. We have paid the premium promptly till date.

Kindly depute your surveyor to see for himself the extent of loss. Subsequently, we will lodge a claim with full details.

Thanking you,


Yours faithfully,
Ravi Nayak
The Personnel Manager
Hindustan Spices Ltd.


SS-MV

***

## <u>Letter to Insurance Company- Request for Group Insurance</u>

# Diamond Cement Ltd

## Maihar Road Katni (MP) 395003
### Phones-076-23435429, 30,31,32,33, Fax-076-234354650, 51, 52,53
### E-mail – diamondcement@rediffmail.com
### Visit us on diamondcement.com

19 May, 2003
Reference- P – Ins – 550

**The Manager**
**United India Insurance Company**
**Rashmi Vihar Ashoka Road**
**Jabalpur 340003**

Dear Sir,

Subject: Group Insurance required

We are a state-of-the-art cement company located at Katni in central India. We employ a total of 250 persons covering different cadres.

It is our interest to take insurance to cover different possible hazards. In this connection, we request you to depute your senior official to hold discussions with the undersigned and make suggestions regarding the type of policies we can take and the amounts thereof.

Thanking you and looking forward to the visit.

Yours faithfully,


Sarita Das
The Personnel Manager

Diamond Cement Ltd.

RKP-MS

***

## <u>Letter to Insurance Company-Request for Group Medical Insurance</u>

# Sarala Cement Works Ltd.

**Rewa Road Maihar (MP) 392003**
**Phones-075-23435429, 30,31,32,33, Fax-075-234354650, 51, 52,53**
**E-mail – saralacementworks@rediffmail.com**
**Visit us on saralacementworks.com**

5 March, 2003
Reference- P – Ins – 54

**The Manager**
**Vindhya Insurance Company**
**Rashmi Vihar Ashoka Road**
**Rewa 487009**

Dear Sir,

Subject: Group Medical Insurance required

We are a cement company with our state-of-the-art plant located at Maihar  in central India in the state of Madhya Pradesh. We employ a total of 250 persons covering different cadres.

We wish to take group medical insurance covering all our employees and all of their family members. In this connection, we request you to depute your senior official to hold discussions with the undersigned and make suggestions regarding the type of policies we can take and the amounts of premium thereof.

Thanking you and looking forward to the visit.

Yours faithfully,


Chitra Singh
The Personnel Manager
Sarala Cement Works Ltd.

MK-SDS

*** 

# Part 10

# *Interoffice Correspondence*

*This Part
Contains
The Memos
That
Are
Written
To
People
Within
The
Organization*

# Inter-office Correspondence

Besides external communication that takes place between different organizations, there is another form of formal correspondence that takes place within the organization between different people of an organization. It is known as Inter-office Correspondence. In other words Inter-office Correspondence is formal written correspondence between two persons / offices of the same organization. It is popularly known as Interoffice Memo or Interoffice Memorandum or a memo in short. In simple words, we can say that it is a short piece of writing generally used by the officers of an organization to communicate among themselves besides keeping a record of the same. A memo may be used for a short request, conveying any information or decisions or conveying a short report.

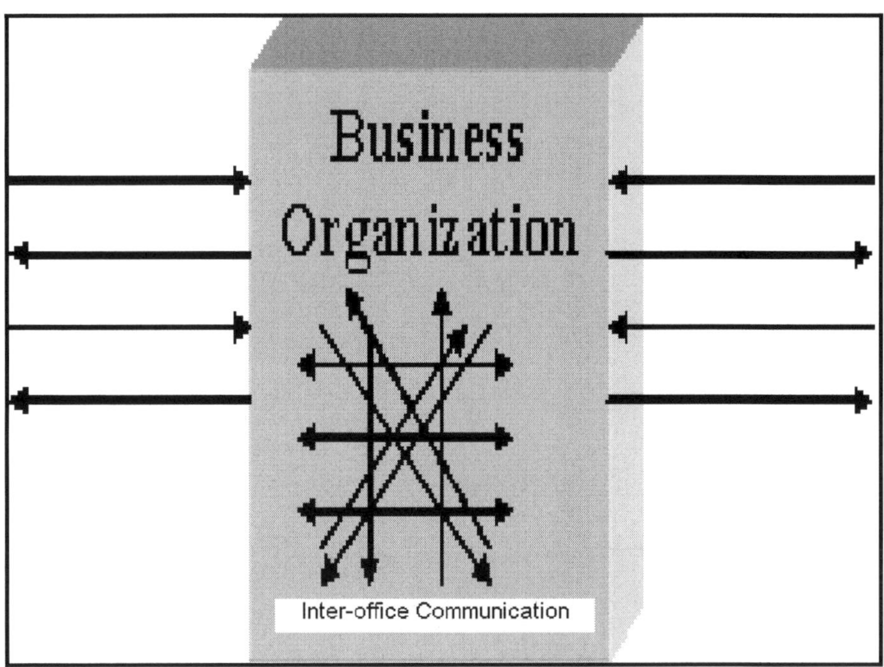

Many organizations use printed memo and one can quickly write the information on it and convey the information to the concerned officer. In comparison to a letter it takes particularly very less time to write a memo because it has less details and formalities.

It has the following elements which are essential for a memo.

        (i)     The designation of the receiver
        (ii)    The designation of the sender
        (iii)   Reference
        (iv)   Date
        (v)    Re: or Subject
        (vi)   Main Body
        (vii)  Copy to (CC)
        (viii) Signature

Each organization has its own way of arranging the various parts of a memo. One should follow the pattern prevalent in one's organization.

# Swastika Cement Limited
## Maihar Road Katni (MP)
### Inter-office Memo

To: The Purchase Manager     Reference: S F – 034

From: Sales Manager                     12 May 2004

Subject – Requirement of office furniture

The sales executive of Chhatarpur city has reported that they need 10 office chairs and 20 stools for their office because the number of customer visit has doubled since April 2004. Please arrange for the purchase of 10 office chairs and 20 stools for Chhatarpur office.

c.c. Sales Executive
     Chhatarpur                     Raghwendra Mishra

# Sarita Cables Limited
Birla Road Satna (MP)
## Inter-office Memo

Reference: S F – 034
12 May 2004
To: The Personnel Manager
CC: Managing Director
From: The Manager Production
Re : Conflict Resolution Required

A conflict between Assistant Manager Production Mr. Suraj Prasad Pandey and Senior Engineer Ravish Kumar Jain has been reported to my office from both the parties. I have tried my best from my side to resolve it but all my attempts have failed. I request you to intervene in the matter and reach a resolution. I am afraid that the continuation of conflict may result into termination or suspension of either of the parties.

Rajendra Tiwari

## Exercise 5

1. Assume yourself to be Ravi Varma the Purchase Manager of Black Diamond Cement Ltd. Satna. Write a letter to Laxmi Furniture Ltd New Delhi inviting quotation for office chairs, almirah, tables and stools.

2. As the Sales Manager of Nixo Fans Ltd. Mumbai write a letter sending quotation for 100 fans to Sawastika Cement Ltd Satna (MP)

3. As the Purchase Manager of  Sawastika Cement Ltd Satna (MP) place the order for 100 fans with Nixo Fans Ltd,Mumbai.

4. Assuming yourself to be Ravi Varma the Purchase Manager of  Black Diamond Cement Ltd. Satna. Write a letter of complaint to Laxmi Furniture Ltd New Delhi that you have received some damaged furniture.

5. Assuming yourself to be the Sales Manager of Laxmi Furniture Ltd New Delhi, write a letter of adjustment to the Purchase Manager of Black Diamond Cement Ltd. Satna. They have received some furniture in damaged condition.

6. As the Purchase Manager of Jetking Cables Ltd., write a letter inviting quotation of 10 air conditioners to CMP Air Conditioners Ltd. New Delhi.

7. As the Purchase Manager of Jetking Cables Ltd., write a letter of complaint to CMP Airconditioners Ltd. New Delhi that some of the AC's have only mild cooling.

8. As The Sales Manager Orpat Fans Ltd. Chennai, write a letter of adjustment to The Purchase Manager Swastika Cement Ltd. Satna (MP). They have received a short supply of 2 fans.

9. As The Manager HRD Laxmi Steels Ltd Satna (MP), write a letter of inquiry to Bhushan Steels Ltd Bhubaneswar Odisha, requesting them to send you information about their security policy that they are applying to prevent accidents in the factory.

10. As the Purchase Manager of an esteemed firm, write a letter to CMP Air-Conditioners requesting them to buy 10 air conditioners or credit purchase basis. Invent necessary details by yourself.

11. Assume yourself to be The Sales Manager of CMP Air-Conditioners Gurugram (Haryana). A firm named Savita Traders New Delhi has requested you to buy 10 air conditioners on credit purchase basis. Write a reply accepting their request for credit purchase.

12. Assume yourself to be The Sales Manager of Corona Fans Ltd. Chennai, a firm named Shaista Traders Hyderabad has requested you to buy 20 fans on credit purchase basis. Write a reply refusing to sell on credit purchase basis.

13. Assume yourself to be The Sales Manager of CMP Air-Conditioners Gurugram (Haryana). A firm named Savita Traders New Delhi purchased 10 air conditioners on credit purchase basis but they did not pay on time as promised by them. Write a collection letter reminding them of the balance pending with them.

14. Assume yourself to be The Sales Manager of CMP Air-Conditioners Gurugram (Haryana). A firm named Savita Traders New Delhi purchased 10 air conditioners on credit purchase basis but they did not pay on time as promised by them. Even after two reminders they have not heeded to your warnings. Write a final warning letter that you are handing over this case to your lawyer.

15. Assuming yourself to the Purchase Manager of Sarala Cables Ltd. Jabalpur, write a letter to Swift Automotive Ltd Mumbai inviting quotation for five light commercial vehicles. Invent necessary details by yourself.

16. Assuming yourself the Sales Manager Swift Automotives Ltd. Mumbai, write a letter sending quotation to the Purchase Manager of Sarala Cables Ltd. Jabalpur (MP).

17. Assume yourself the Purchase Manager Sarala Cement Maihar Satna (MP). You placed an order for lubricant for your plant with Slide Lubricants Mumbai. But when your Store Manager received the consignment, he found 6 cans of lubricants broken and lubricant leaked. Write a letter of complaint.

18. Assume yourself the Sales Manager Slide Lubricants Mumbai. You received a letter of complaint from Sarala Cement Maihar Satna (MP) stating that six of the lubricant containers were found broken and the content leaked. Write a letter of adjustment.

19. Assume yourself the Purchase Manager of a famous cement company. The Sales Manager of your company wanted some furniture for Chhatarpur office. Write an interoffice memo to the Sales Manager of your company that the order for their required furniture has been sent.

20. Assume yourself to be the sales manager of Truba Gensets Ltd. New Delhi. You have recently started producing state-of- the- art gen sets for various commercial and domestic uses. Write a sales letter to Shraddha Hospital and Nursing Home Satna (MP) describing the special features of your genset.

21. Assume yourself to be the Accounts Manager of Luxury Footwears Ltd. New Delhi. You need a loan to start a new footwear production unit at Kanpur. Write a letter to the Branch Manager State Bank of India Dariyaganj New Delhi requesting to grant you a loan of Rs. 3000000=00 (Thirty lakh) against your property and goodwill.

22. Assume yourself to be the Accounts Manager of Kohinoor Soaps and Detergent Ltd. Jabalpur. Write a letter to the Branch Manager State Bank of India Russel Chowk Jabalpur requesting him to increase your overdraft limit from Rs. 1000000=00 to Rs 1500000=00, (from Rs. Ten lakh to Rs. Fifteen lakh).

23. Assuming yourself to be the Accounts Manager of Luxury Footwears Ltd. New Delhi, write a letter to the Branch Manager State Bank of India Dariyaganj New Delhi asking him the reason of dishonouring your cheque of Rs. 300000=00 (Three lakh).

24. Assume yourself to be the Accounts Manager of Luxury Footwears Ltd. New Delhi. Recently, your showroom at Daryaganj New Delhi caught fire and a lot of shoes along with your showroom were charred in fire. Write a letter to the Manager United India Insurance Shahdara requesting him to send an agent to assess the damage.

25. Assume yourself the Sales Manager Slide Lubricants Mumbai. You have overall 120 employees in your organization. You want medical coverage for all your employees and their family members. Write a letter to Reliance Insurance Ltd. Shahdara New Delhi inviting quotation for medical insurance.

# Part 11

# *Social Correspondence*


*This
Part
Contains
How
To
Write
Invitation
To
Marriage*

# Social Correspondence

These letters are written with a view to fulfilling social obligations or meeting social needs. These letters include invitation to any social function and condolence letter. It is in fact an informal letter that you have already read. If you write a letter to anyone inviting him to a social function or if you write a condolence letter, it is social correspondence done by using the format of informal letter. But nowadays, people don't write letters but get the invitation printed by using a different format. You have already come to know how to write an informal letter. You can write this letter easily. You can see the sample of such invitation in an informal letter is shown here :-

10 Rajendra Nagar

Jabalpur

19 May 2017


Dear Mr. and Mrs. Awasthi ji,

Could you please give us the pleasure of your company at Dinner at 7 PM at Hotel Deepak on 25 May 2017? We are hosting dinner to celebrate 25th anniversary of our marriage. Your honorable presence is eagerly solicited.

All the staff members have been invited.

With best wishes


Yours sincerely,

Mrs Shraddha Shrivastava

Mr. Pawan Shrivastava

Nowadays, printed marriage invitations are quite common and several formats with different style and content are available with the printers. One can choose the one suitable for their purpose. There is no hard and fast system. All is conventional. You can break the custom and design invitation according to your culture and tradition. However, some samples are given below.

# Sample 1. Printed Marriage Invitation

Dr. Mahesh Kumar Singh

And

Mrs. Shalini Singh

Request the honour of your company

At the marriage of their daughter

## Shweta Singh

(granddaughter of Ramesh Kumar Rawat)

With

## Mr. Harish Singh

(son of Shree Shailendra Singh and Shreemati Neeta Singh)

On 17 May 2017 in the evening(7PM)

At Hotel Sakshi Priyam Bazar Indore

With best compliments from
Mr. Satish Kumar Singh
And
Mrs. Reeta Singh

Together with their family

# Adam Smith
And
# Ivana Smith

Invite you to celebrate
The joy of their wedding day

Sunday 25 October
4.30 in the afternoon

At Hotel Shereton Mumbai

**Useful and Important Sentences**
**Invitations**
1.    You are cordially invited to our wedding celebration.
2.    We would be delighted if you could join us for dinner.
3.    Please join us for a baby shower in honor of (Name).
4.    We are hosting a garden party and would love to see you there.
5.    You are invited to our annual holiday gathering.
6.    Please save the date for our anniversary celebration.
7.    We hope you can attend our housewarming party.
8.    Join us for a special evening of fun and festivities.
9.    Your presence would make our event even more special.
10.                    We are excited to invite you to our family reunion.
Congratulatory Messages
1.    Congratulations on your new job!
2.    Well done on your recent promotion.
3.    Wishing you all the best in your new home.
4.    Congratulations on your engagement!
5.    I'm so happy for you on your graduation.
6.    Best wishes on your retirement.
7.    Congratulations on the birth of your baby.
8.    You did an amazing job, congratulations!
9.    I'm thrilled to hear about your success.
10.                    Congratulations on your anniversary!
Condolences
1.    I am deeply sorry for your loss.
2.    My thoughts and prayers are with you during this difficult time.
3.    Please accept my heartfelt condolences.
4.    I am here for you if you need anything.
5.    Wishing you peace and comfort during this tough time.
6.    My deepest sympathies go out to you and your family.
7.    May the memories of (Name) bring you comfort.
8.    I am so sorry to hear about your loss.
9.    You are in my thoughts and prayers.

10.	May you find strength in the love and support of friends and family.

# Part 12

# *Email Writing And Business Email*

*This Part
Contains
How to Write Email
And
Use of Email For
Business Correspondence*

# Email (Electronic Mail)

As I have already mentioned in the beginning, the frequency of letter writing has decreased due to Email. Email is the product of the internet which is the World Wide Web of computers in which it is very easy to send a message to one or some or to all computers in the web instantly. The company that provides Email service is known as Email Service Provider (ESP). There are several email service providers, more than 400 in the world. Mostly it is free of charge facility but some business email services are chargeable also. Some famous Email Service Providers are Gmail, Rediff, Yahoo, and Hotmail etc. You can open the home page of any of these ESP's and go in for 'sign up' or 'create new account' and follow the instructions and you can create your Email account. Now you are ready to send and receive emails from and on your account.

# Popularity of Email

Email has now become one of the most popular means of information sharing. It has pervaded the whole world. It came into existence in late twenties and it has clearly outperformed letter writing in almost every field. Now it is impossible to imagine correspondence without emails. These are some valid reasons behind the popularity of email:-

**Emails are easy, fast and cheap:** - Emails are easy, cheap and fast to use. An email practically takes no time to reach the destination. Besides this you can attach a huge amount of data and many files with your email which will cost you almost nothing. Most of the Emails are free of charge.

**Emails reflect scientific temper:** -Science and technology have contributed speed and sophistication to our lives and emails are very much befitting to the spirit of science and technology. There are different types of technologies to take care of different aspects of our life. So is the email to take care of our correspondence.

**Emails do many things automatically:-**Science and technology have made people impatient not only regarding getting their message but in composing their message also. We get our message fast and we adapt to various short cuts while composing our messages especially the ones which are informal. Emails do many things automatically which set our tone and style and which a letter can never do.

## Emails are valid and legal

Though starting informally, emails are now regarded as valid and tenable proof to some one's claims legally. After all it is a written message which cannot be altered or denied. Besides this, the technology can also inform us whether the message has been delivered and whether it has been attended or not.

# Drawbacks of Email

Although there are several advantages from email, we must not forget that there are several pitfalls associated with the emails e.g.

**Your Email is not Personal and Private:-**Since emails are sent through an internet facility, a system administrator can always reach our emails, read them and disclose them to others. Emails are prone to hacking also.

**People tend to become casual with Email:-**Due to enormous popularity and its availability on cell phones, emails by their nature breed informality and casualness. Besides this, there is no universally acceptable methodology of writing emails. The result is that people are writing in the manner they like. But all this is blurring the line between formality and informality which is not good. Therefore we should be careful and use formality and informality judiciously.

## Using shortcut forms of words arbitrarily: -

People tend to use short forms of words arbitrarily. Sometimes this casualness makes the message difficult to understand or it may be ambiguous. People may not mind it in informal communication but for formal communication, we must make our message clear and meaningful. The convenience that email has provided us has taken away the virtue of the language. People have become habitual of writing shortcut, racy, pushy and jerky language. For informal emails it may be right but for formal writings it is not advisable.

## Unwanted Messages:-

Email accounts receive a lot of unsolicited emails and spams. They crowd the mailbox due to which one may miss an important mail. Besides this, since emails can be sent with the click of a button, you may get unrelated messages because you are a part of an organization and a part of an email service provider organization so you get all the related and unrelated mails.

# Guiding Principles for using Email for Formal Writings

Since Email provides several facilities, we must be careful in writing formal emails. The following guiding principles may help:-

## Don't be abrupt:-

Don't be in a haste to write everything in short  like informal email or messaging. Your message may be too short and lack clarity. Be clear with all the necessary details.

## Don't forget to use the subject line:-

Formal emails must include a subject line. Emails do provide this facility therefore use it effectively.

**Don't forget courtesy:** -Courtesy is like oil which removes friction. It fills energy in our relationship that is why it is an important element of formal letters and informal letters too. Remember that writing an email without courtesy may be rude. Use salutation and complimentary close like the ones used in business letters. Many a times, we get good news but we forget to respond by our thanks. The first sentence must be of thanks if you are writing a reply.

**Using all capitals is a bad habit:-** Sometimes people don't care that they are writing in all capitals. They think that it will make their message attractive but it is not a good habit. It will actually mar the beauty of your message.

**Avoid Acronyms:** - Since people habitually use shortcuts in emails; they resort to self-made acronyms which may make your formal writing unintelligible and annoying. Therefore, acronyms are to be avoided. However, you can use acronyms which are currently in use and people are aware of them.

**Don't use emoticons and smileys:** - Formal communication does not require emoticons or smileys. They should be avoided in business communication.

**Mind the punctuation of writings:** - Formal communication is not casual writing therefore it must have proper punctuation marks. Even in informal writings, punctuation makes it clear and understandable.

**Identify yourself properly:** - Don't use abbreviations to identify yourself. Write clearly who you are along with disclosing your designation.

# Business Email

When we use Email for business communication, it is known as Business Email. There is no doubt that like informal communication; the use of Email in business communication too has increased tremendously.

Business email is a crucial part of modern business correspondence. It is a fast, efficient, and professional way to communicate in the corporate world. Compared to traditional business correspondence (such as letters and memos), business emails offer several advantages:

## Key Features of Business Email:

1. **Speed and Efficiency** – Emails are delivered instantly, making communication faster than traditional letters.

2. **Cost-Effective** – Unlike printed letters, emails do not require paper, postage, or delivery services.

3. **Convenience** – Emails can be sent from anywhere, making remote communication seamless.

4. **Record Keeping** – Emails provide a written record of communication, useful for tracking agreements and decisions.

5. **Global Reach** – Emails can be sent to anyone worldwide in seconds.

6. **Attachments and Formatting** – Business emails allow users to attach documents, images, and links, adding more depth to communication.

# How Business Email is Different from Traditional Business Correspondence:

# How Business Emails Improve Business Correspondence:

- **Faster decision-making** due to instant responses.
- **Increased productivity** by reducing wait times.
- **Eco-friendly** as it reduces paper usage.
- **More interactive** with hyperlinks, multimedia, and attachments.

# Business Email in Modern Correspondence

## 1. Introduction

- Definition and importance of business email.
- How it has transformed business communication.
- Comparison with traditional business correspondence.

## 1. Definition and Importance of Business Email

## 1.1 Definition of Business Email

A business email is a formal and professional electronic message exchanged between individuals, companies, or organizations for official communication purposes. Unlike casual emails, business emails follow a structured format and maintain a professional tone. They are used for various purposes, such as inquiries, negotiations, proposals, orders, complaints, and official updates.

## 1.2 Importance of Business Email

1. **Speed and Efficiency** – Business emails enable instant communication, reducing delays in decision-making and project execution.

2. **Cost-Effective** – Unlike postal mail, emails eliminate the need for paper, printing, and postage, cutting operational costs.

3. **Professionalism** – Emails provide a formal and structured way to communicate, ensuring clarity and credibility.

4. **Record-Keeping** – Business emails serve as a written record of agreements, transactions, and communications for future reference.

5. **Global Accessibility** – Emails allow businesses to connect with clients, partners, and employees worldwide without geographical barriers.

6. **Convenience and Flexibility** – Business emails can be sent and accessed from anywhere, enabling remote communication and work collaboration.

7. **Security and Confidentiality** – Emails can be encrypted and protected to ensure sensitive business information remains secure.

8. **Multifunctionality** – Attachments, links, and multimedia elements make emails versatile for various business needs.

# 2. How Business Email Has Transformed Business Communication

## 2.1 Evolution of Business Communication

Before the advent of email, business communication relied on letters, faxes, and telephone calls, which were time-consuming and expensive. The introduction of business email in the 1990s revolutionized corporate interactions, making communication faster and more efficient.

## 2.2 Key Ways Business Email Has Transformed Communication

1. **Faster Decision-Making**

- o Traditional correspondence took days or weeks, whereas emails deliver messages instantly.

- o Quicker responses lead to more efficient business operations.

## 2. Improved Documentation and Record-Keeping

- o Emails provide a permanent digital record of conversations, eliminating the need for physical storage.

- o Searchable archives help retrieve important information effortlessly.

## 3. Enhanced Collaboration

- o Emails allow teams to work together across different locations.

- o File-sharing, project updates, and virtual meetings are now seamlessly integrated with email communication.

## 4. Greater Customer Engagement

- o Businesses can instantly respond to customer inquiries and complaints.

- o Automated responses and email marketing strategies improve customer relations.

## 5. Environmental Impact

- o Reduced reliance on paper and physical mail services has made business communication more eco-friendly.

## 6. Flexibility and Remote Work

- o Employees can communicate and work from anywhere, increasing productivity and efficiency.

- o Mobile email access has further enabled work on the go.

7. **Integration with Other Digital Tools**

- o Emails are now integrated with calendars, CRM software, task managers, and cloud services, making workflows smoother.

# 2.3 The Shift from Traditional to Digital Communication

## Conclusion

Business email has revolutionized the way organizations communicate, making interactions faster, more cost-effective, and more efficient. It has enhanced collaboration, improved documentation, and enabled businesses to operate on a global scale with ease. As technology advances, business email will continue to evolve, integrating with AI and automation for even greater efficiency.

# The Key Components of a Business Email

- **Sender and Recipient Fields** (To, CC, BCC) The 'To,' field is for main recipient of the letter. This field eliminates the need of 'Inside Address' that is used in the traditional Business Correspondence. You can send different copies of the same letter to different recipients using 'CC,' as we do in the traditional business correspondence. You can put certain recipients in the 'BCC,' field like you send Blind Courtesy Copies ( BCC ) to certain recipients in traditional Business Correspondence.
- **Date** – It is automatically printed in the email.

- **Subject Line** – Like in traditional Business Correspondence, you have to write a subject line to make correspondence clear and relevant. It should be concise and clear limited to one line only.
- **Salutation** – You can use formal or informal greetings depending upon whether you email is a formal or informal one.
- **Email Body** – You have to write Email Body like the Main Body of traditional Business Correspondence You should structure the content with clarity, conciseness and professionalism.
- **Closing and Signature** – You have to close the letter like the complimentary close of traditional Business Correspondence The element Signature of the traditional Business Correspondence becomes Email Signature in Business Email. It eliminates the need of Letter Head as used in traditional Business Correspondence. An example of Email Signature is given below:-

Instead of a letterhead, an email typically ends like this:

Best regards,
John Smith
Sales Manager | XYZ Corporation
📞 (123) 456-7890 | ✉ john.smith@xyz.com
🌐 www.xyzcorporation.com

This serves the same purpose as a letterhead by providing all essential contact information.

# Key Differences from Traditional Business Letters:

1. **No Need for a Letterhead:**

    o In traditional business letters, a letterhead includes the company name, logo, and contact details at the top.

o In an email, this information is usually found in the **email signature** at the end of the message.

2. **No Inside Address Required:**

o A traditional letter includes the recipient's full address below the date.

o In an email, the recipient's details are already in the **"To"** field, making an inside address unnecessary.

# What Replaces These in an Email?

# Email Structure vs. Letter Structure

## Here I present six well-structured business email examples: -

### 1. Email Inviting Quotation

**To -** recipient's email.com

**Subject:** Request for Quotation for Office Supplies

Dear [Supplier's Name],

I hope this email finds you well. We are looking to procure office supplies for our company and would appreciate it if you could provide a quotation for the following items:

- [List of items with specifications]

Kindly include details regarding pricing, payment terms, delivery time, and any bulk order discounts. We would appreciate receiving the quotation by [Deadline Date].

Looking forward to your prompt response.

Best regards,
 [Your Name]
 [Your Position]
 [Your Company Name]
 [Your Contact Information]

## 2. Email Sending Quotation

**To -** recipient's email.com

**Subject:** Quotation for Office Supplies – [Company Name]

Dear [Client's Name],

Thank you for your inquiry regarding our office supplies. Please find attached our detailed quotation for your requested items.

**Key Details:**

- **Total Cost:** [Amount]
- **Payment Terms:** [Specify]
- **Delivery Time:** [Specify]
- **Discounts:** [Mention if applicable]

Please review the attached quotation and let us know if you have any questions or require further clarification. We look forward to your order.

Best regards,
 [Your Name]
 [Your Position]
 [Your Company Name]
 [Your Contact Information]

(Attachment: Quotation.pdf)

## 3. Email for Placing an Order

To - recipient's email.com

**Subject:** Purchase Order for Office Supplies

Dear [Supplier's Name],

Thank you for your quotation dated [Date]. We are pleased to place an order for the following items as per the terms outlined in your quotation:

**Order Details:**

- [List of ordered items with quantity and price]
- **Total Amount:** [Amount]
- **Delivery Address:** [Specify]
- **Preferred Delivery Date:** [Specify]

Please confirm receipt of this order and provide an estimated shipping date. The payment will be processed as per our agreed terms.

Best regards,
[Your Name]
[Your Position]
[Your Company Name]
[Your Contact Information]

(Attachment: Purchase_Order.pdf)

## 4. Email for a Complaint Letter

To - recipient's email.com

**Subject:** Urgent: Complaint Regarding Defective Products

Dear [Supplier's Name],

I am writing to formally bring to your attention an issue regarding our recent order #[Order Number] received on [Date]. Unfortunately, we noticed that [describe issue, e.g., defective, incorrect, or damaged products].

We request an immediate resolution to this matter, either through replacement or a refund. Please let us know how you would like to proceed to rectify this issue.

Looking forward to your prompt response.

Best regards,
[Your Name]
[Your Position]
[Your Company Name]
[Your Contact Information]

(Attachment: Photos of damaged items)

## 5. Email for an Adjustment Letter (Response to Complaint)

**To** - recipient's email.com

**Subject:** Apology & Resolution for Your Complaint – Order #[Order Number]

Dear [Customer's Name],

Thank you for bringing this matter to our attention. We sincerely apologize for the inconvenience caused by the issue with your recent order #[Order Number].

To resolve this, we are offering [mention solution: replacement, refund, discount, etc.]. The replacement items will be shipped by [Date], and we will ensure this does not happen again.

We appreciate your patience and value your business. Please feel free to reach out if you need further assistance.

Best regards,
 [Your Name]
 [Your Position]
 [Your Company Name]
 [Your Contact Information]

## 6. Sales Letter Email

**To -** recipient's email.com

**Subject:** Exclusive Offer: [Product/Service Name] to Boost Your Business

Dear [Customer's Name],

We are excited to introduce our latest [Product/Service], designed to help [benefit to customer, e.g., improve efficiency, reduce costs, increase sales].

**Why Choose Us?**
✔ [Key Benefit #1]
✔ [Key Benefit #2]
✔ [Key Benefit #3]

As a valued customer, we are offering an exclusive [Discount/Free Trial/Promotion] valid until [Date]. Don't miss this opportunity!

Let's discuss how our solution can benefit your business. Feel free to reply or call us at [Contact Number].

Looking forward to working with you.

Best regards,
 [Your Name]
 [Your Position]
 [Your Company Name]
 [Your Contact Information]

(Attachment: Product_Brochure.pdf)

Printed in Great Britain
by Amazon